The Encyclopedia of Tubular Bead Crochet

Ann Benson

Edited by Barbara Ponticelli

ISBN 979-86895524-5-3

Czech copper-lined light amethyst AB 8°s crocheted
6-around on Conso nylon with caps. rondelles, spacers,
and amethyst focal bead, with a spring-clasp closure

For Charlotte
Miss you, Baby Dog

Czech and Japanese 11°s in a diamond
pattern crocheted 8-around (**8-07**) on
Cebelia 30, with Swarovski pearls and crystal
rondelles in a roll-on closure

Contents

Czech and Japanese 11°s on Cebelia 30
crocheted 8-around (**8-32**) with caps, crystal
beads, spacers and a separating magnetic clasp

What's it all about?

Tubular bead crochet is simply a spiral of slip stitch with a bead captured in each stitch.

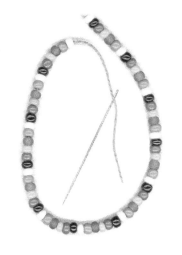

Beads are threaded in specific patterns onto crochet thread.

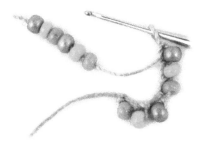

A foundation of beaded chain stitches is crocheted.

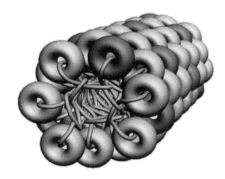

Slip stitches with beads are worked into all the beaded chains. Slip stitches with beads are worked into all previous slip stitches until the tube is the desired length. There is a hollow interior (a tube) of fibers with the beads on the outside.

How tubular bead crochet differs from beaded single crochet

Single beaded crochet (also called tapestry bead crochet) is worked from a charted design, in the round, with a step-up at the end of each round. This technique is often used for beaded purses and creates a substantial and strong beaded "fabric."

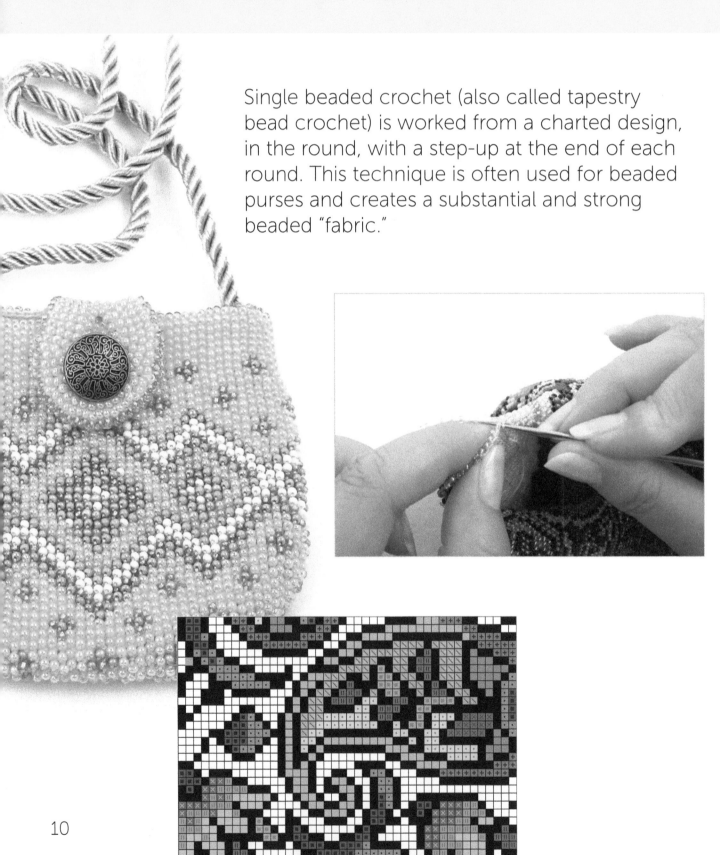

How tubular bead crochet differs from double bead crochet

Double bead crochet, also called Euro or harness bead crochet (a translation error, it's said) is a spiral technique like tubular bead crochet, but stitched in the single crochet stitch instead of slip stitch. There is no step-up in this technique; the spiral continues until the desired length is reached. The resulting tube is quite open and usually requires support within the channel to maintain a smooth outer appearance. Because the beads are slipped at a different point in the stitch, they slant differently than in simple tubular bead crochet. Design possibilities are more intricate, but it takes more time than tubular bead crochet.

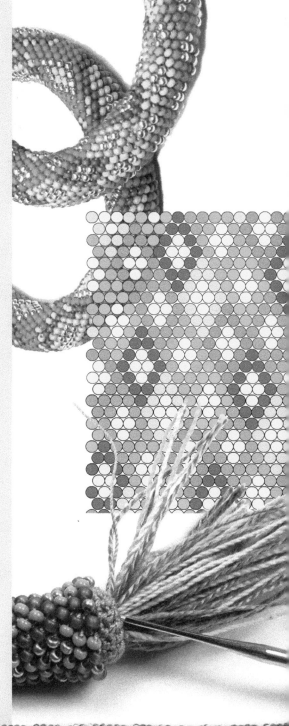

In double bead crochet (above) note how the beads are slanted on the diagonal. In tubular bead crochet (below) the beads are perpendicular to the length of the tube

First there are beads.

You may already be familiar with seed beads. But if you're a beginner, these guidelines can help you choose beads.

Where they're made and how they're shaped will determine how your tube looks.

Czech Republic seed beads include Jablonex and Preciosa brands. They're rounded in shape and have smaller holes than Japanese beads. Because of their softened shape, they crochet beautifully; Czech bead tubes bend more sinuously than those made entirely from Japanese beads. Color numbers are roughly standardized between brands, though distributors often assign their own numbers.

Japanese seed beads include Toho, Miyuki and Matsuno. Toho and Miyuki beads are very similar in size, slightly larger than Czech, but smaller than Matsunos. Both Miyuki and Toho have consistent, large holes and result in tubes with consistent surfaces and diameters. Matsunos have the largest holes; their 15° seed beads crochet wonderfully. Color numbers are not consistent between Japanese brands.

Brands can be mixed; I regularly mix Japanese and Czech beads of the same size and different sizes. That said, if you want absolute consistency in your tube's appearance, using one brand alone can yield a flawless appearance.

Size does matter.

From small to large, these are the most popular seed beads for tubular crochet. Of course you can use other shapes and sizes such as cubes, triangles, and small drops. Experiment!

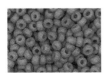 **Japanese 15°s** (1.3 x 1.5 mm) Miyuki and Toho are the same size, Matsunos tend to have slightly larger holes. Starting a tube can be a challenge but after a couple of rounds they're wonderful. Huge color range and good availability.

 **Czech 12°s** (1.9 x 1.4 mm) slightly larger than Japanese 15°s. They crochet beautifully and make very fluid tubes; limited availability of color range.

 **Japanese cylinder beads** (1.6 x 1.5 mm) (Delicas, Aikos/Treasures). Size 11 is standard, but they are also available in size 15 (1.3 x 1 mm). Squared edges; tubes can be a bit rigid. Large holes; huge color range, readily available.

 **12° three-cuts** are made in both Japan and the Czech Republic. Their sparkle makes them an excellent bead for embellishment within a larger pattern. Their holes are often small, so try a floss threader. Limited color availability.

 **Czech 11°s** (2 x 1 mm) have rounded edges and are more elliptical in shape than Japanese, so tubes made entirely from this type of bead will have the most bend and flexibility. Amazing color range, very good availability.

 **Japanese 11°s** (2.1 x 1.1 mm) have larger holes then Czech and their edges are generally more squared. Tubes made entirely from Japanese 11°s are very neat and consistent in appearance. Thousands of colors, great availability.

 **Czech 8°s** (3x 2 mm) have rounded edges and good-sized holes. These are the best beads to use when learning. Tubes work up quickly and are substantial in diameter. Great color range, especially in metallics, good availability.

 **Japanese 8°s** (3.1 x 2.1 mm) are also great for learning. They are slightly larger and more squared than Czech and create a neat, consistent tube with good fluidity. Excellent color range, easy availability.

 **Japanese and Czech 6°** (4 x 3 mm) seed beads are quite varied in size within brands. It's not recommended to learn on this size as their weight makes them hard to handle. Great for necklaces. Availability and color range are both good.

And then thread.

Your strong, stable, high quality thread has to fit through the bead holes. And it should be pretty. Here are some recommended combinations, but there are many manufacturers who make their own brand of threads that are suitable. As long as the bead fits onto the thread, feel free to experiment with any non-stretching thread. Sizes are listed from small/fine to heavier/thicker.

Thread	Beads
30/2 cotton or silk	Czech 13°, Japanese 15°, 15° three-cuts
Gutermann Topstitching Mettler Jean Stitch	Czech 13°, Japanese 15°, 15° three-cuts, 12° three-cuts, Czech 12°, Czech 11°
Heavy-duty buttonhole	15° three-cuts, 12° three-cuts, Czech 12°, Czech 11°
Size 30 Cebelia™	15°, 12° three-cuts, Czech 12°, Czech 11°
Size 20 Cebelia™	12° three-cuts, Czech 12°, Czech 11°, Czech 10°, Czech 9°, Czech/Japanese 8°
Size 12/2 perle coton	Czech 11°, Czech 10°, Czech 9°, Czech/Japanese 8°
Size 8/2 and 10/2 perle coton	Czech 10°, Czech 9°, Czech/Japanese 8°, firepolish rounds, rondelles, small crystals
Size 5/2 perle coton	Czech/Japanese 8°, Czech/Japanese 6°, firepolish rounds,
Size 8/2 tencel rayon	Same as 8/2 perle coton (this thread shrinks when wet but regains size when dry)
Metallic braided fibers	Any clear/translucent bead that will fit over the fiber

And there are tools.

Suggested steel crochet hooks for beads/threads

You'll adjust your hook according to your own stitch tension and the specific beads/threads you're using, but this is the basic range of hooks needed for tubes.

Hook size	Threads	Bead sizes
13/14 .9 mm	30/2 cotton/silk, Gutermann	15°, 12°, 11°
11/12 1.0 mm	Cebelia 30/20, Gutermann, Conso, 30/2 cotton/silk	15°, 12°, 11°
10/ 1.15 mm	Cebelia 30 and 20. Gutermann, Conso, Perle cotton 10/2, 8/2	12°, 11°, 10°, 9°, 8°
9/ 1.25 mm	Cebelia 20, Gutermann, Conso, Perle cotton 10/2, 8/2	11°, 10°, 9°, 8°, 6°, decorative/larger beads
8/ 1.4 mm	Gutermann, Conso, Perle cotton 12/2, 8/2, 5/2, metallics/braids	10°, 9°, 8°, 6°, decorative and larger beads

Use any threading device that will accept the thread and fit (threaded) through your beads. I use these below.

Threading device	Bead sizes	Threads
Dental floss threader	Any size bead	All threads
Size 12 beading needle	15°, 12°, 11°	30/2 cotton/silk, Gutermann
Size 10 embroidery needle (excellent for 11°s, widely available)	Some 15°, 12°, 11°, 10°, 9°, 8°	Cebelia 30 and 20, Gutermann, Conso, Perle cotton 10/2
Size 10 beading needle	12°, 11°, 10°, 9°, 8°	Gutermann, Conso, Perle cotton 10/2
Size 9 darning needle	Some 11°, 10°, 9°, 8°, decorative/large beads	Gutermann, Conso, Perle cotton 10/2, 8/2, 5/2

Wet the end of the thread and compress it flat, then cut it at a clean angle. Now wet the eye of the needle. The threading will be easier!

Preparing to crochet

It's so much easier if you do a few simple things beforehand.

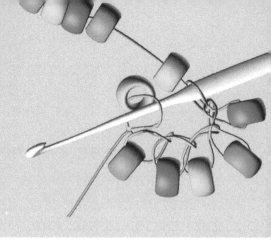

For a true beginner, the recommended size of beads is 8°, with size 10/2 perle coton thread (yes, this is the correct spelling of this French-born fiber but "pearl cotton" is generally used, and a size 9 steel (1.25mm) crochet hook. The recommended tube circumference for learning is six-around. If possible, choose six distinctly different (opaques recommended) colors for your first project; using six colors will facilitate self-assessment as your tube grows. You can use three colors and repeat them twice within each round, but to be absolutely certain you're crocheting correctly, six colors work well.

Thread management is always an issue; use a winding card roughly the size and shape shown here. Cereal box cardboard will work nicely. The two holes are where you will store your work when you set it aside; by inserting the hook in one hole and the blunt end in the other, you secure the beaded thread and the crocheted tube quite safely.

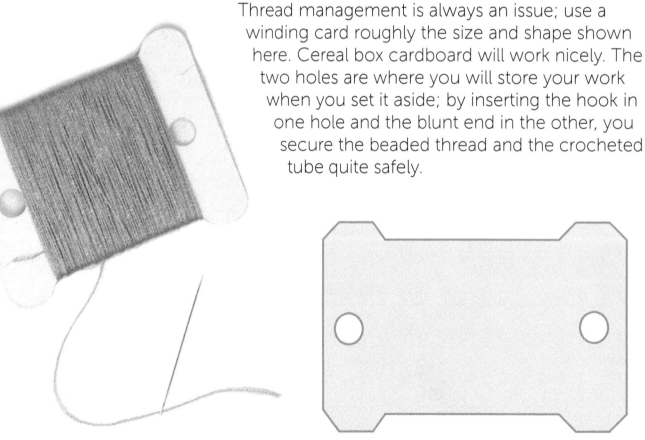

Threading

Threading a simple pattern is easy if you lay out your beads in pattern order in small separated piles. Thread consistently from one side to the other. The first bead threaded is the last bead crocheted.

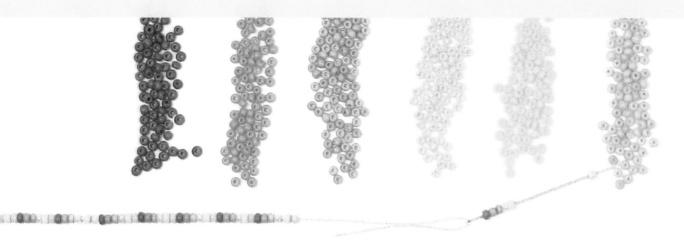

Czech opaque/lustered 8°s are used here with a neutral color thread. The threading device is a size 9 darning needle.

Pick up one bead of each color in order from left to right, then start again with another group in the same order from left to right.

For a seven-inch bracelet, you need about seventy rounds of beaded crochet in size 8° beads. More about sizing later, to help you plan your own designs.

Unwind a few yards of thread and push the beads down, so they aren't all in one packed line. I often leave the needle on the end of the thread until I've established the start of the tube, as it weighs down the starting thread tail and keeps it out of the way. And it's handy if you're burying your starting thread as part of finishing.

Actually crocheting

Every tube's foundation is a chain of beads. A tube of six-around is shown here; all tubes are started in this manner regardless of the number of beads per round.

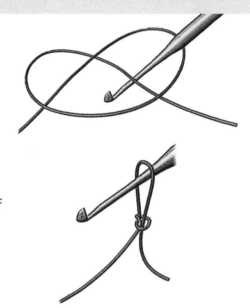

A beaded chain forms the foundation of your tube. Chain stitch starts with a slip knot. Chains are counted AFTER the slip knot; it does not become a stitch in and of itself. Form your thread into a pretzel as shown, then insert the hook under the thread and pull up a loop. Tighten the loop onto the hook by pulling on the free end, leaving a tail of about six inches. You may want to use this tail later depending on the finishing technique you choose.

With the slip knot in place, the first bead is brought down the thread to nestle against the knot. The thread is wrapped over the hook from back to front.

The thread is caught in the hook and pulled through the slip knot to form the first chain.

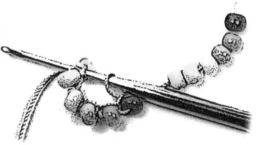

The remaining beads of the foundation round are chained in the same manner. Note how the chain has already started to arc. You are now ready to begin the subsequent rounds, which will be built on this foundation chain.

Continuing

Each stitch after the foundation consists of five distinct steps. The steps remain the same through the completion of the tube.

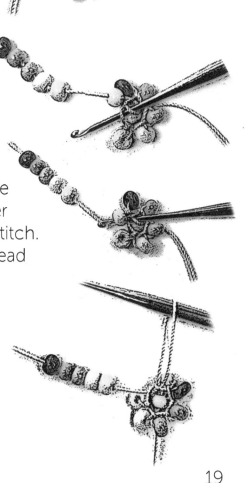

IN

Insert the hook **IN** the loop that holds the bead of the first beaded chain. Do not pierce the thread or run through the bead hole. Insert the hook only into the chain loop itself.

OVER

Push the bead **OVER** the hook so it's on the outside of the hook, away from you.

DOWN

Reposition the beaded thread as shown; move the tail out of the way. Bring a new bead **DOWN** the thread so it nestles against the hook.

AROUND

Wrap the thread over and **AROUND** the hook so the thread lays to the right of the bead you pushed over the hook; this step is critical to the success of the stitch. You now have two loops on your hook and the thread is wrapped.

THROUGH

Pull the wrapped thread **THROUGH** both loops on the hook. The bead appears to be in the center of the foundation, but as more stitches are added it will move out to the edge of the tube.

The whole point is to create a crocheted slip-stitch spiral tube with fibers on the inside and beads on the outside.

These are the five steps in each stitch that will create the spiral beaded tube, the tubular bead crochet mantra! As long as you don't deviate from this progression of steps, your tube will be a success.

IN
OVER
DOWN
AROUND
THROUGH

The bead you pushed over the hook

The carrying thread to the right of the bead

The new bead ready to be secured

The thread that carries the bead MUST be positioned to the right (or left, if you are left-handed) of the bead that you pushed over the hook. The simple act of pushing the bead over the hook positions it on the outside of the tube. Wrapping and pulling the thread through the loops secures the new bead to the previous round and puts it in the right position for the NEXT round.

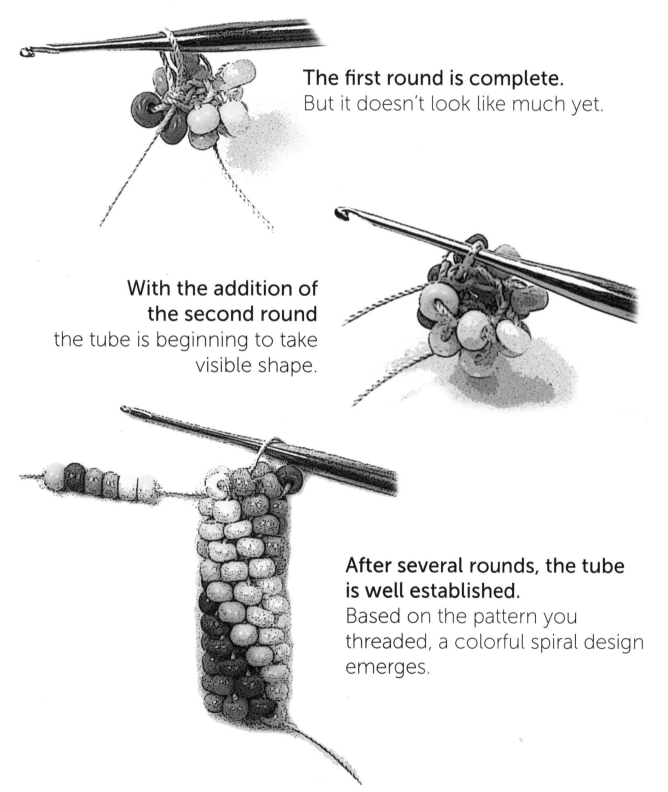

The first round is complete.
But it doesn't look like much yet.

With the addition of the second round the tube is beginning to take visible shape.

After several rounds, the tube is well established.
Based on the pattern you threaded, a colorful spiral design emerges.

The anatomy of a tube

The overall pattern, in this case a six-color spiral, becomes more evident with added length.

This seven-inch tube in 8° seed beads, crocheted six-around, has 76 full rounds in a repeating pattern of six colors which form a spiral when correctly threaded and correctly crocheted.

The starting end rarely looks lovely, especially when you're a beginner. This end shows the thread tail and the first round of beads, all in the "donut" position.

The beads of the main tube are positioned like donuts, with the holes less visible because they are covered with the beads directly above and below

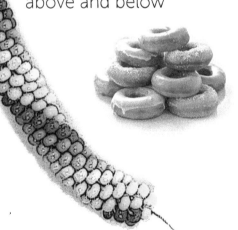

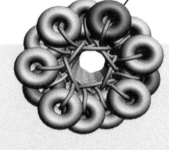

The channel shown in this graphic is exaggerated, but all crocheted tubes do have a threaded channel that runs the entire length of the tube. In certain finishing techniques you may need to run some sort of element like a wire, a fiber bunch, or a chain through this channel, so it's always wise to keep it as clear as possible.

As you progress, the top round beads will always be positioned like tires, upright with the holes visible

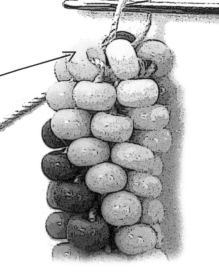

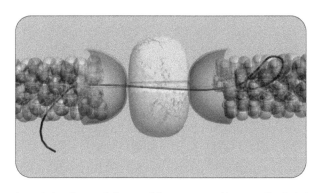

When all the beads are crocheted, the top round beads will STILL be in the tire position. If you are planning to finish your tube with an invisible join (more on that later) you will leave the end round just like this.

If you're planning almost any other type of finishing, it's probably a good idea to crochet one round of slip stitch without any beads. Doing so will reposition the beads into the donut position.

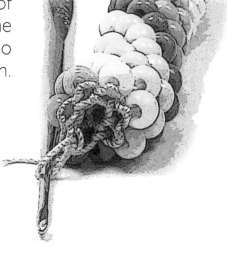

In this focal bead/caps roll-on finishing, the beads at both ends of the tube are in the donut position which makes it easier to control their position within the caps in a balanced manner

Uh oh.

Everything's not perfect.

Beads are landing in the center of the tube.

This is common and almost expected at the very start of a tube. But in an established tube, it's trouble. The most likely reason: you are not following the cardinal rule that the carrying thread MUST come from the right (or left if left-handed) of the bead you pushed over the hook. This is the single most common reason why crocheted tubes fail.

An errant bead has migrated to the center of the tube

In this graphic the bead you pushed over the hook is shown in red. The new bead is light green. Note how the carrying thread comes from the right side of the red bead. This is critical to the success of the stitch. To fix this problem, pull out stitches to the location of the errant bead and rework them. MAKE SURE you have the correct loop on the hook before you start crocheting again.

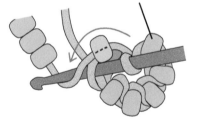

PULL ON THIS BEAD TO CHECK

If it's not the correct loop, everything you've crocheted before that stitch will pull free when the tube is first stretched. With the hook in the loop you've picked up, pull on the bead of the prior stitch; if it's secure, you're in the right loop. If it pulls free, try again to find the right loop. The tip of a needle may work better than the hook.

You started with one number of beads in circumference and now you have a different number.

Most likely it's a smaller number, as it's more common to drop a stitch than to add one. It also happens more frequently when you're crocheting in just one color without pattern. There's no solution for this other than to pull out stitches until you have the correct number and start again. To avoid this, flatten the top of your tube from time to time and count the beads in the top round.

Your tube is lumpy or wavy.

Getting to the "Goldilocks" place can take some experimentation with the three components of beads, thread and hook. Try stitching eight or nine rounds with your chosen components before fully threading the pattern; if you're not happy with the result, adjust the components. Stitch tension can also play a major role in tube consistency.

9-around tube in Czech 11°s on 20/2 cotton with 1.10 mm hook

9-around tube in Czech 11°s on Cebelia 30 cotton with 1.25 mm hook

Loose tension creates loops that are too large; the bead moves on the loop and shifts position. The bead may pop into the center of the tube; in extreme cases, the thread loop will actually cross over the bead of the previous round, resulting in a very annoying knot. If you can't correct loose tension with a concentrated effort, a smaller hook may be your solution. For example, if you're working in size 8° seed beads with a size 9 steel hook (1.25mm), try a size 10 steel hook (1.10 mm).

Tight tension often happens when you first learn. You're struggling to use all the fingers of both hands harmoniously, so tenseness is normal. You'll find it difficult to insert the hook into the loop because the thread is rigid. After a couple of projects, your tension may loosen naturally. If you're happy with the look of your tubes, great! But if tight tension does not correct itself with developing skills, you can switch to a larger hook size.

Uneven tension There is no specific method for correcting this beyond paying attention. Again, this often occurs in new learners. Over time, your stitching will take on a rhythm, your hands will develop "muscle memory" for the five steps of each stitch. Tubular bead crochet will start to feel like swimming or riding a bicycle, just something that you do. This is when it truly becomes fun.

Threading complex patterns

When you're threading a pattern with multiple rows for each repeat, laying out piles in order may not be a good method. That said, there are a few things you can do to make it easier to stay in pattern.

Establish a first repeat that is absolutely accurate. Check it at least three times against the printed pattern to be sure that it's perfect. Make note of the number of beads in the repeat. Use this first repeat as a standard against which you compare subsequent repeats. You can tape the first repeat to a rigid surface like a small piece of cardboard to keep it stable for easier comparison, but pull out enough thread to add subsequent repeats before taping the initial pattern in place.

These two repeats of the pattern are correct and identical.

There are errors on the second repeat shown below. On quick glance, the repeat may appear longer or shorter, indicating too many or too few beads. The errors become evident on closer inspection and can be corrected before additional repeats are added.

THIS BEAD IS MISSING IN THE SECOND REPEAT

THERE ARE TWO EXTRA BEADS

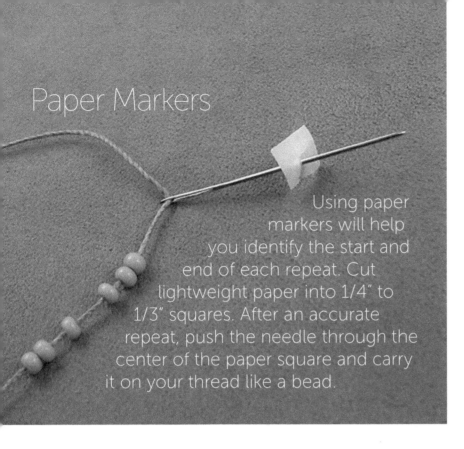

Paper Markers

Using paper markers will help you identify the start and end of each repeat. Cut lightweight paper into 1/4" to 1/3" squares. After an accurate repeat, push the needle through the center of the paper square and carry it on your thread like a bead.

Paper markers placed between repeats of a pattern will help you count the repeats. You can also use paper markers to indicate the location of "events" such as increases and decreases.

Adding in a new thread

You may need to add a new thread if you've made a significant mis-threading and you have to cut the thread to correct it. You may also opt to load beads in sections for very long projects.

Pull a loop of the new thread through the last loop of old thread. To hold the loops, wrap masking tape (NEVER duct tape) around the thread tails. Bring a bead down the new thread and crochet as if it were the old thread. After several rounds, remove the tape and secure the tail within the fibers of the tube.

Correcting a threading error

Mistakes happen, and if you didn't catch it in threading, you'll need to correct it mid-tube. If you have an extra bead, PUT ON EYE PROTECTION, then place the bead on a hard flat surface that can't be damaged (I use a bamboo cutting board). Place the tip of your hook into the hole of the bead and press down quickly. The bead will explode outward, hopefully leaving your thread intact. If you have missed a bead, you have two options: make an unbeaded slip stitch in the position of the missing bead, treat it as a beaded stitch in the next round. Go back later and sew in the correct bead. Or you can cut the thread, add the missing bead, and pull the new thread into the crochet as described above.

Choosing bead colors

Precise color recommendations are not given in this book.
Specific beads go in and out of supply daily; some go out of
production permanently. You can spend your life chasing down a
particular bead. And you would not be able to lift this book for all
of the pages that would be required. So here are tips for making
your own grown-up beader choices. Do not be afraid.

Contrast, contrast, contrast.
Patterns will not emerge unless there is sufficient
difference in the value of the colors used. The
two identical-pattern bracelets shown at right
each have three colors. Both have the same
opaque pale lavender and opaque dark blue;
one has a transparent metallic copper, the other
opaque metallic copper. Note how the stripes of
transparent copper seem to disappear into the
crochet, while the opaque bead is clearly visible.

**Transparent beads will take on the color of the
thread.**
This is actually quite a lovely thing when you plan it.
This red metallic braid shines through the transparent
light topaz AB beads. If you combine opaque and
transparent colors in one project, the transparent
beads will be modified by the thread color; the
opaque will retail their original color. The results can
be stunning!

This simple bracelet was stitched on
variegated 8/2 tencel in size 8° crystal
clear seed beads. The shading is soft
and pretty. Try coloring your thread
with permanent markers!

The numbers

Note that these numbers WILL vary according to your stitch tension, manufacturer, and hook size. It's always wise to overestimate; it's easier to remove unneeded beads than to add more.

How many rounds?

15° = 21-24 rounds per inch
12° = 19-20 rounds per inch
11° = 16-17 rounds per inch
11 cylinders = 19-20 rounds per inch
10° = 15-16 rounds per inch
9° = 14-15 rounds per inch
8° = 12-13 rounds per inch
6° = 9-10 rounds per inch

How much thread?

Your thread's manufacturer will indicate the number of yards per gram. Each slip stitch takes at least of one-half inch of thread. A six-around 8" long tube requires up to 10 yards/meters. Wind more thread than you think you'll need.

How many beads?

15° = 275 beads per gram
11 cylinders = 190 beads per gram
11°/12° = 90-100 beads per gram
10° = 80 beads per gram
9° = 70 beads per gram
8° = 40-50 beads per gram
6° = 15-25 beads per gram

Wait! You don't have a gram scale.

Use the half-teaspoon rule instead. One-half teaspoon has roughly the following number of beads per size:

15° = 800
11 cylinder beads = 675
12° = 540
11° = 400
10° = 300
9° = 190
8° = 150
6° = 56

For example:

You're using a seven-around pattern in 11°s to make an 8" tube.
7 x 16 rounds per inch = 112 rounds
7 beads x 112 rounds = 784 total beads

Your pattern repeat has twelve beads, 4 of color A and 8 of color B.
784 divided by 12 = 65.3 repeats
65.3 x 4 = 261.3 beads of color A (2.6 grams, less than one-half teaspoon)
65.3 x 8 = 522.6 beads of color B (5.2 grams, less than one full teaspoon)

One-half inch x 784 = 392 inches, divided by 36 = 10.88 yards of thread

Using the patterns

Patterns are grouped by the number of beads in the tube's circumference. Five beads in each round is the generally the smallest practicable circumference to achieve a discernible design. Ten-beads rounds offer great design possibilities, but that is the point at which the tube may begin to collapse inward on itself; you may need to use a fiber bundle, piping cord or rubber cord to support the rounded shape (finishing, later pages).

The top of each section page shows the number of beads per round.

The first page of any circumference section includes information for the approximate diameter of tubes in multiple sizes of seed beads.

Patterns contain four graphical items: diagonal overview, 3D rendering, one repeat of the linear pattern, and a bead count needed for an 8" tube of 11°s. These elements will use the same colors in each pattern; the next pattern will have different colors so you can discern them. The layout of patterns may vary depending on the length of the pattern repeat. Most designs will have one line for the repeat; load from left to right.

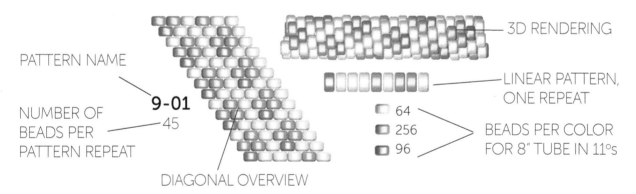

PATTERN NAME

NUMBER OF BEADS PER PATTERN REPEAT

9-01
45

DIAGONAL OVERVIEW

3D RENDERING

LINEAR PATTERN, ONE REPEAT

64
256
96

BEADS PER COLOR FOR 8" TUBE IN 11°s

Where a linear pattern has more than one line, load from left to right, top row first, subsequent rows left to right, top to bottom in order, just as you would read words

Using the patterns continued

Patterns can be used as is or combined. Tubes can also be graduated in circumference, as in the 5-around to 10-around and back example below. Placing your increase or decrease within a solid or striped band will make the size change less visible; placing a circumference change within a repeating pattern can be challenging and not always successful. Personal color choices for pattern beads can be worked out in advance on the "Design your own" blanks, later in the book.

In this necklace, six different patterns (i.e. **5-12**) are combined in graduating/diminuating progression, with increase/decrease (INC or DEC) bands between the patterns. The closure is a simple loop and bead. Threading can start at either end; the design is symmetrical. Increases and decreases (next page) should be made in the center round of the three-round bands.

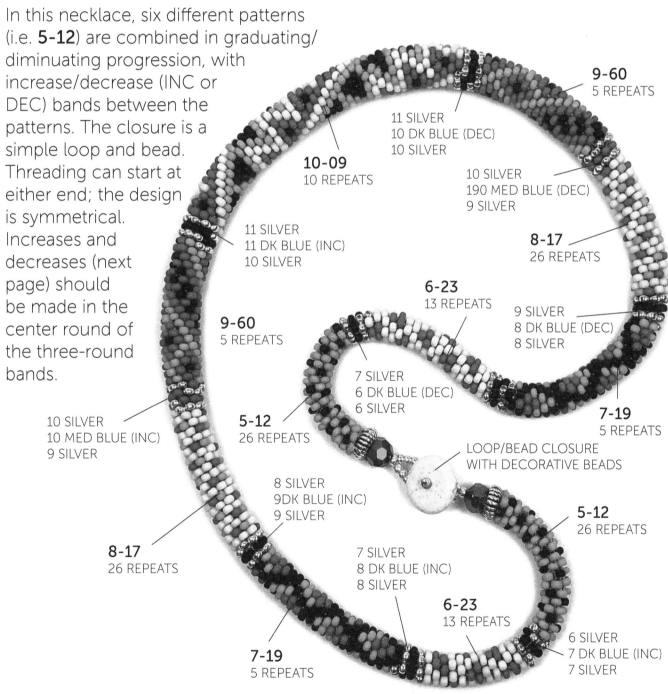

9-60
5 REPEATS

11 SILVER
10 DK BLUE (DEC)
10 SILVER

10-09
10 REPEATS

10 SILVER
190 MED BLUE (DEC)
9 SILVER

11 SILVER
11 DK BLUE (INC)
10 SILVER

8-17
26 REPEATS

6-23
13 REPEATS

9 SILVER
8 DK BLUE (DEC)
8 SILVER

9-60
5 REPEATS

7 SILVER
6 DK BLUE (DEC)
6 SILVER

7-19
5 REPEATS

10 SILVER
10 MED BLUE (INC)
9 SILVER

5-12
26 REPEATS

LOOP/BEAD CLOSURE
WITH DECORATIVE BEADS

8 SILVER
9DK BLUE (INC)
9 SILVER

5-12
26 REPEATS

8-17
26 REPEATS

7 SILVER
8 DK BLUE (INC)
8 SILVER

6-23
13 REPEATS

6 SILVER
7 DK BLUE (INC)
7 SILVER

7-19
5 REPEATS

TO INCREASE IN TUBULAR BEAD CROCHET: Crochet to the position in the tube where the increase should be placed. Make a chain stitch with the next bead, separate from the stitches of the top round. Crochet into the next bead on the top round; do not skip any beads of the top round. The chained bead becomes a new stitch in the top round. When you reach the chained stitch as you progress, crochet into it as you did in the initial chain of your tube. You may find it difficult to insert the hook into the chained stitch, but after the round is completed, the stitch will normalize in tension.

Increases look best when made within a single-color round.

 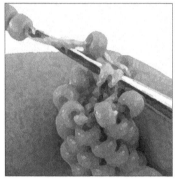 

TO DECREASE IN TUBULAR BEAD CROCHET: This is very easy. Crochet to the point in the tube where the decrease should take place. Make an unbeaded slip stitch at the decrease point, thereby reducing the number of beads in the top round. In the next

round, work only in the stitches with beads; pass right over the unbeaded stitch and continue only in the beaded stitches.

Five-around tube patterns

BEAD SIZE	TUBE DIAMETER
15°	4.9 mm
11-cylinders	5.3 mm
11°	6.2 mm
8°	8.4 mm

DIAMETERS WILL VARY SLIGHTLY BY MANUFACTURER, HOOK SIZE, AND PERSONAL STITCH TENSION

Five-around tubes are thin; they're very quick to thread and crochet. Graphical patterns emerge well; pictorial patterns are less attractive. They're often used for the narrow end of a graduated tube.

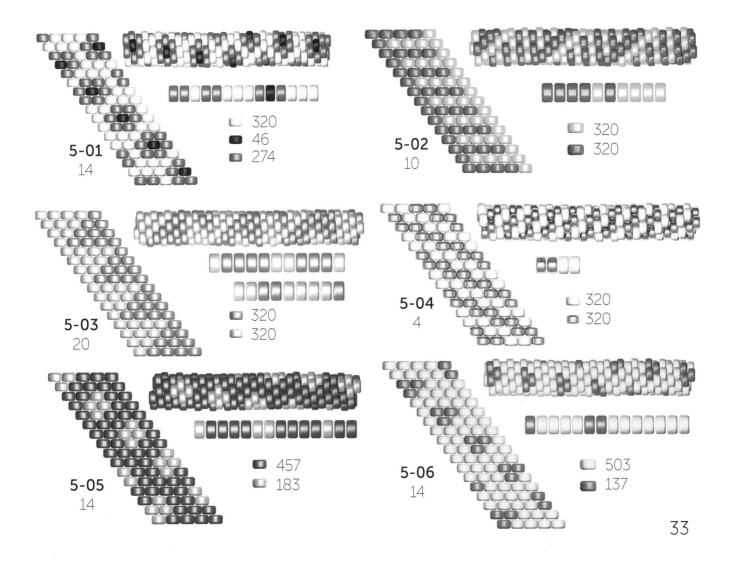

5-01
14

320
46
274

5-02
10

320
320

5-03
20

320
320

5-04
4

320
320

5-05
14

457
183

5-06
14

503
137

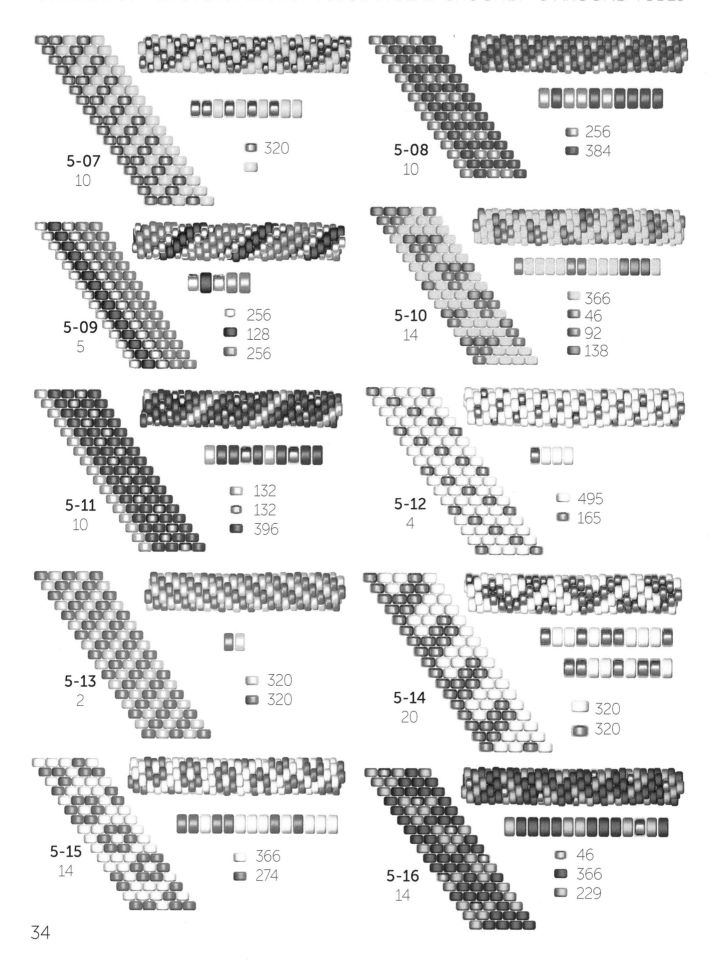

5-07
10

320

5-08
10

256
384

5-09
5

256
128
256

5-10
14

366
46
92
138

5-11
10

132
132
396

5-12
4

495
165

5-13
2

320
320

5-14
20

320
320

5-15
14

366
274

5-16
14

46
366
229

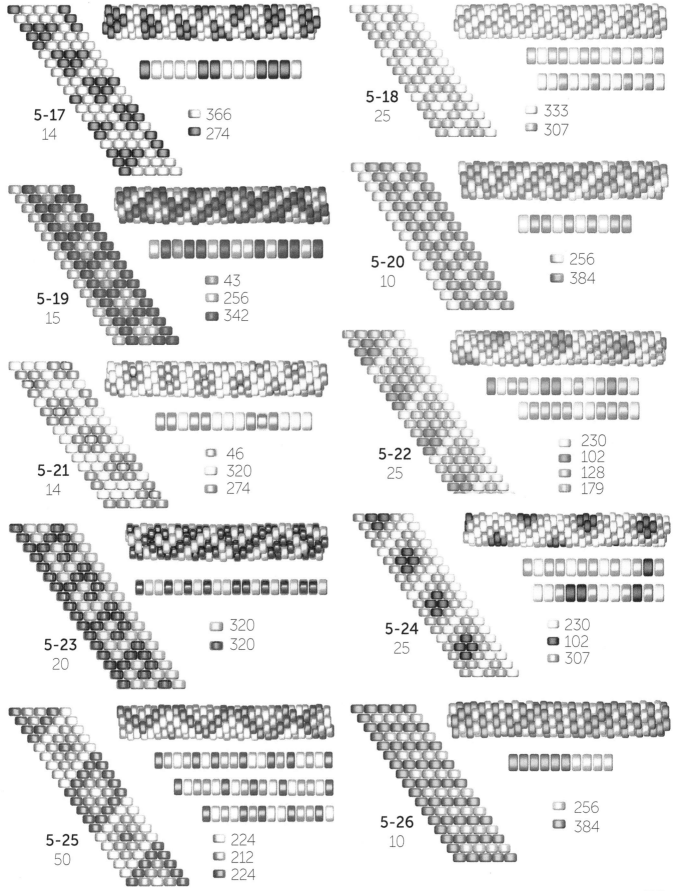

5-17
14

□ 366
◼ 274

5-18
25

□ 333
□ 307

5-19
15

◼ 43
□ 256
◼ 342

5-20
10

□ 256
◼ 384

5-21
14

□ 46
□ 320
□ 274

5-22
25

□ 230
◼ 102
□ 128
□ 179

5-23
20

□ 320
◼ 320

5-24
25

□ 230
◼ 102
□ 307

5-25
50

□ 224
◼ 212
◼ 224

5-26
10

□ 256
◼ 384

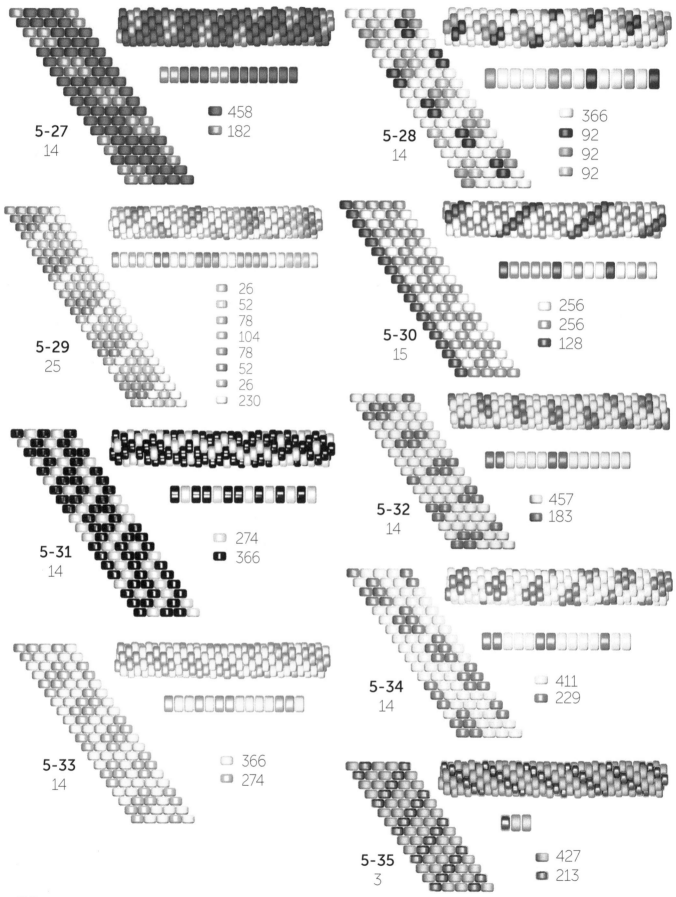

5-27
14

☐ 458
☐ 182

5-28
14

☐ 366
☐ 92
☐ 92
☐ 92

5-29
25

☐ 26
☐ 52
☐ 78
☐ 104
☐ 78
☐ 52
☐ 26
☐ 230

5-30
15

☐ 256
☐ 256
☐ 128

5-31
14

☐ 274
☐ 366

5-32
14

☐ 457
☐ 183

5-33
14

☐ 366
☐ 274

5-34
14

☐ 411
☐ 229

5-35
3

☐ 427
☐ 213

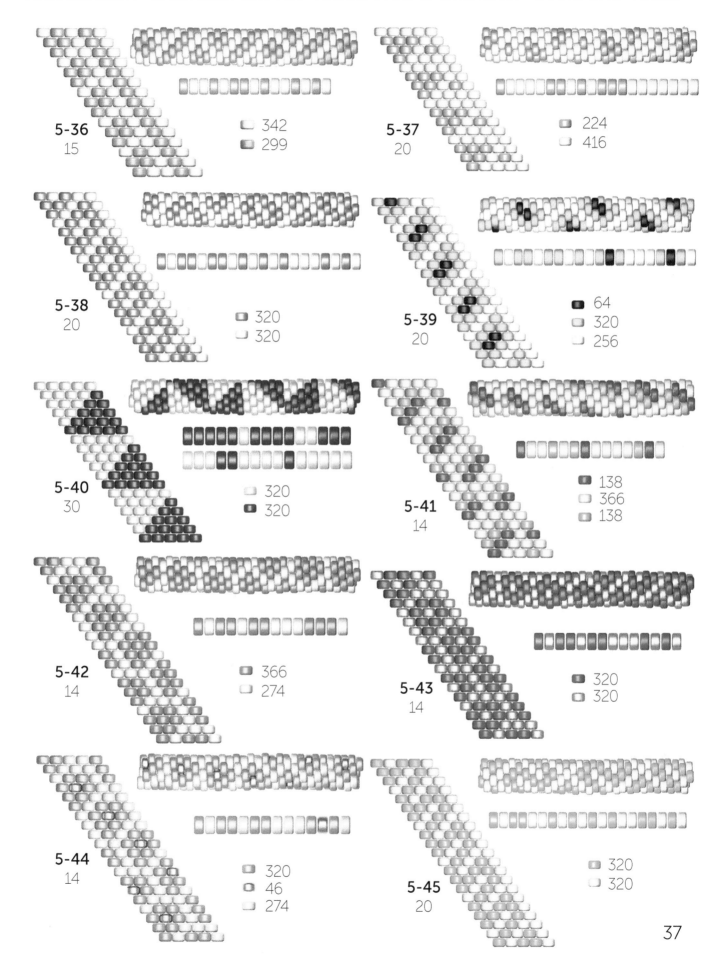

5-36
15
- 342
- 299

5-37
20
- 224
- 416

5-38
20
- 320
- 320

5-39
20
- 64
- 320
- 256

5-40
30
- 320
- 320

5-41
14
- 138
- 366
- 138

5-42
14
- 366
- 274

5-43
14
- 320
- 320

5-44
14
- 320
- 46
- 274

5-45
20
- 320
- 320

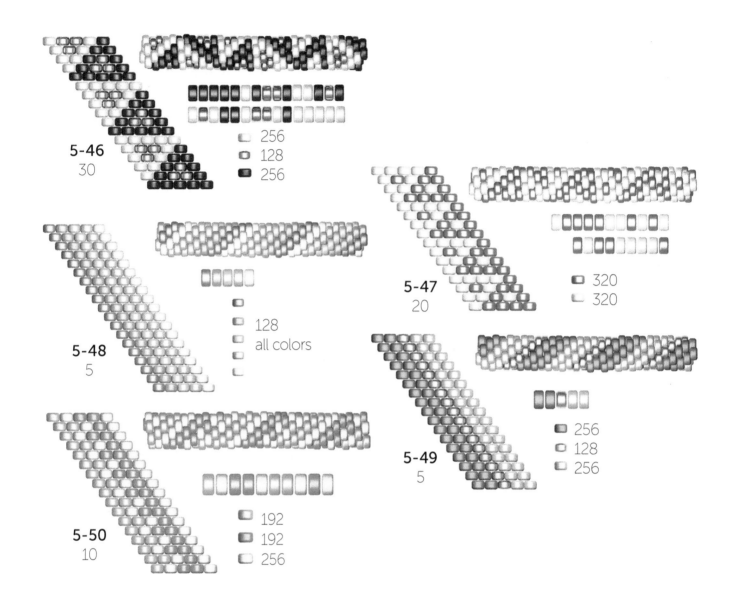

5-46
30

256
128
256

5-47
20

320
320

5-48
5

128
all colors

5-49
5

256
128
256

5-50
10

192
192
256

Six-around tube patterns

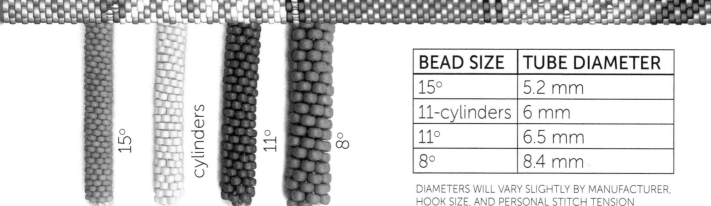

BEAD SIZE	TUBE DIAMETER
15°	5.2 mm
11-cylinders	6 mm
11°	6.5 mm
8°	8.4 mm

DIAMETERS WILL VARY SLIGHTLY BY MANUFACTURER, HOOK SIZE, AND PERSONAL STITCH TENSION

Six-around is fast to thread and stitch; patterns emerge well in this circumference. Graphical patterns are well-defined. Tubes are self-supporting so finishing is generally easy.

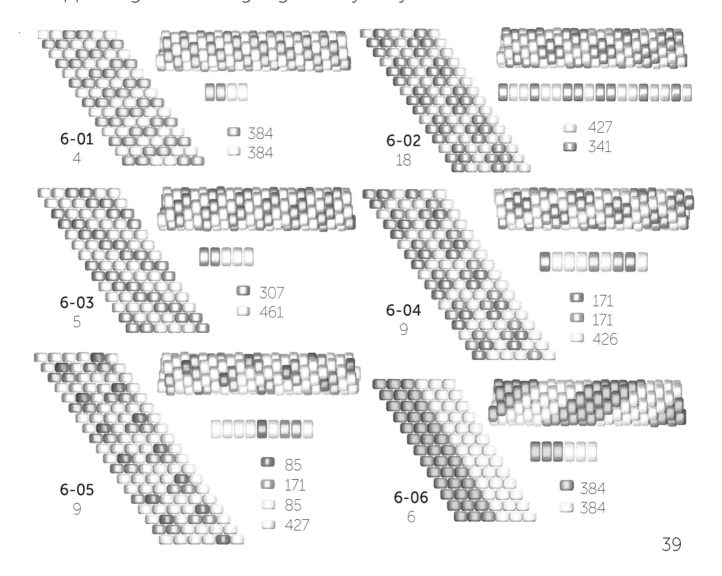

6-01
4
- 384
- 384

6-02
18
- 427
- 341

6-03
5
- 307
- 461

6-04
9
- 171
- 171
- 426

6-05
9
- 85
- 171
- 85
- 427

6-06
6
- 384
- 384

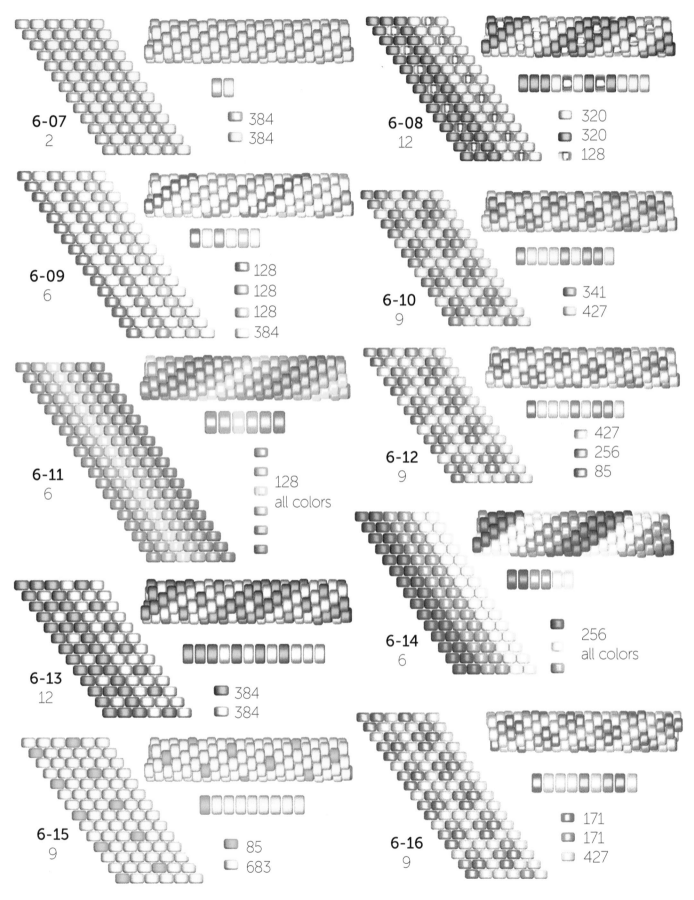

6-07
2

384
384

6-08
12

320
320
128

6-09
6

128
128
128
384

6-10
9

341
427

6-11
6

128
all colors

6-12
9

427
256
85

6-13
12

384
384

6-14
6

256
all colors

6-15
9

85
683

6-16
9

171
171
427

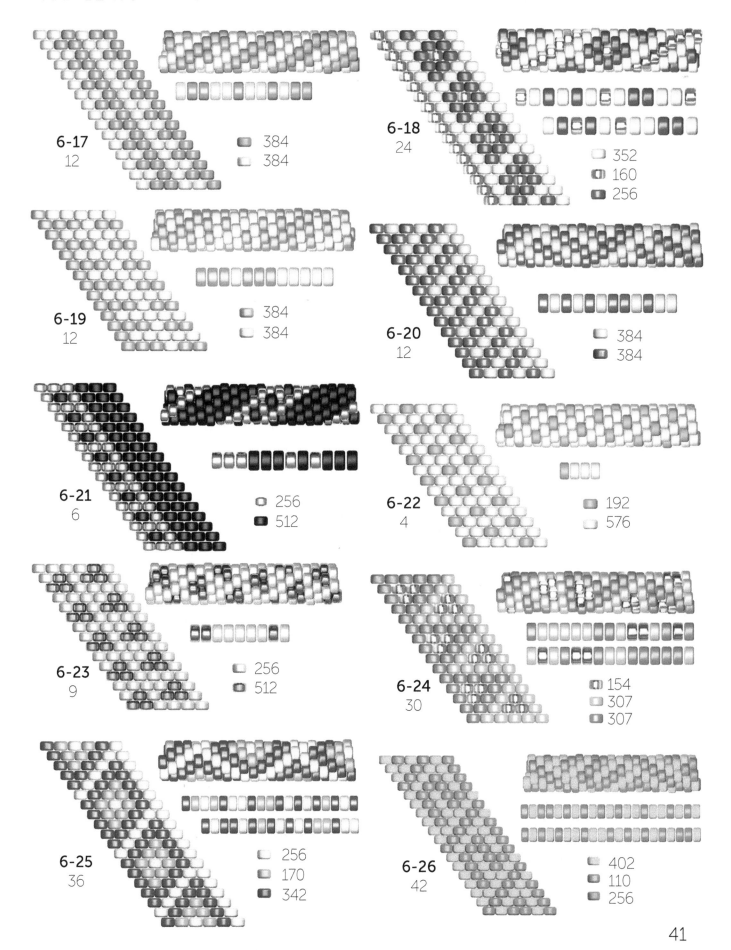

6-17
12

| | 384 |
| | 384 |

6-18
24

	352
	160
	256

6-19
12

| | 384 |
| | 384 |

6-20
12

| | 384 |
| | 384 |

6-21
6

| | 256 |
| | 512 |

6-22
4

| | 192 |
| | 576 |

6-23
9

| | 256 |
| | 512 |

6-24
30

	154
	307
	307

6-25
36

	256
	170
	342

6-26
42

	402
	110
	256

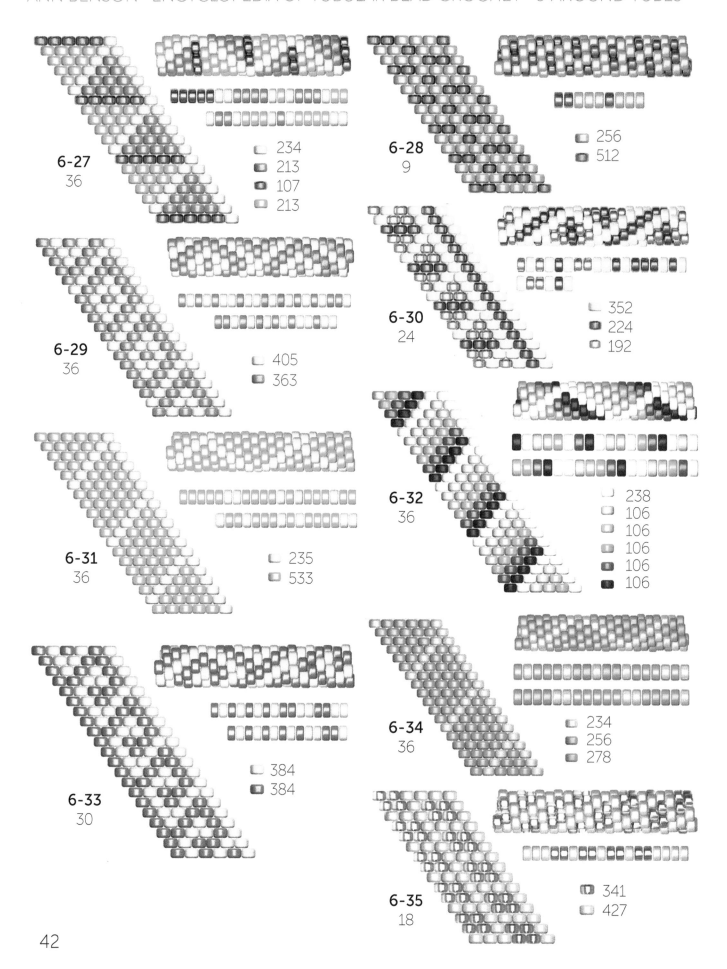

6-27
36

	234
	213
	107
	213

6-28
9

	256
	512

6-29
36

	405
	363

6-30
24

	352
	224
	192

6-31
36

	235
	533

6-32
36

	238
	106
	106
	106
	106
	106

6-33
30

	384
	384

6-34
36

	234
	256
	278

6-35
18

	341
	427

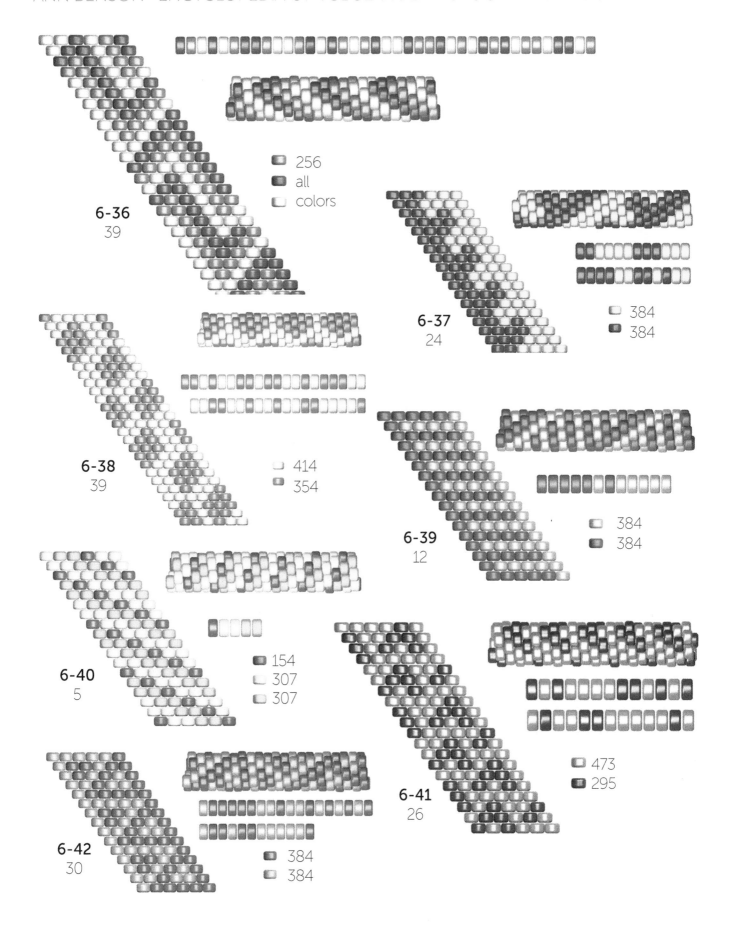

6-36
39

256
all
colors

6-37
24

384
384

6-38
39

414
354

6-39
12

384
384

6-40
5

154
307
307

6-41
26

473
295

6-42
30

384
384

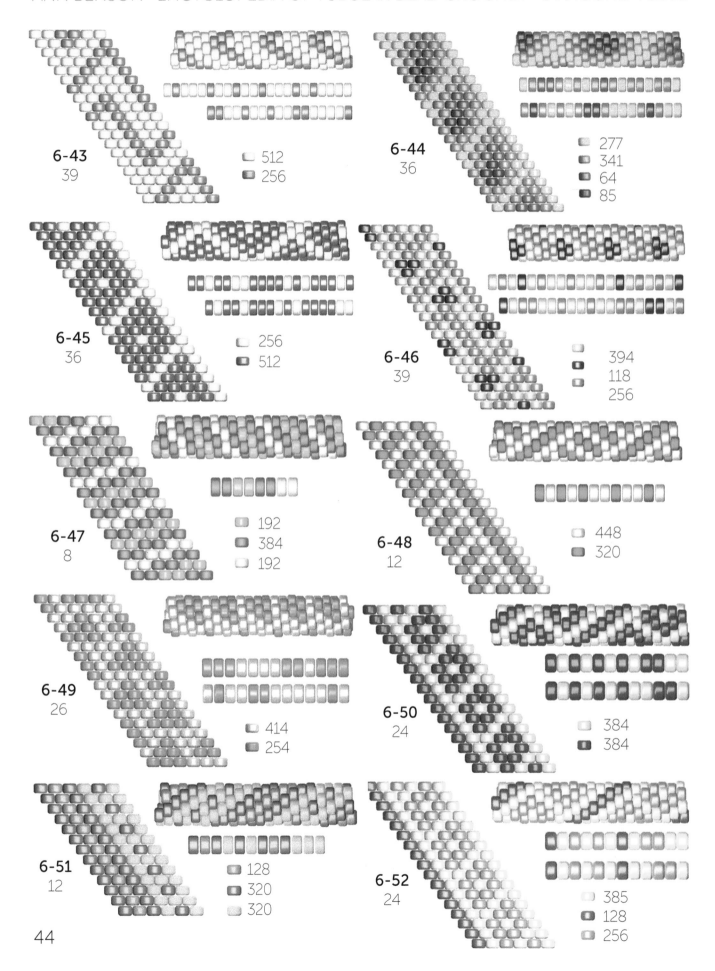

6-43
39

512
256

6-44
36

277
341
64
85

6-45
36

256
512

6-46
39

394
118
256

6-47
8

192
384
192

6-48
12

448
320

6-49
26

414
254

6-50
24

384
384

6-51
12

128
320
320

6-52
24

385
128
256

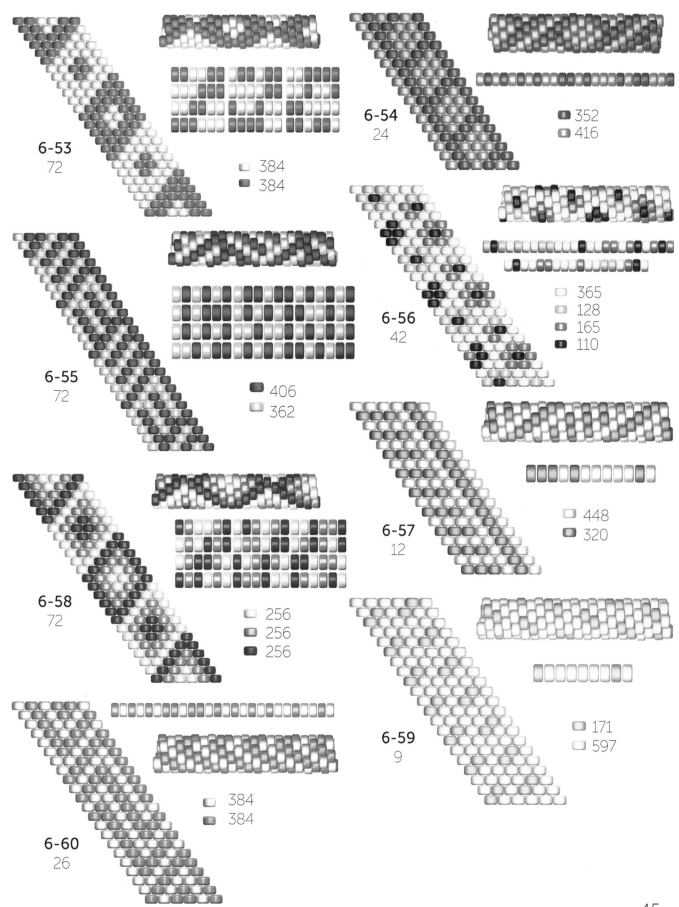

6-53
72

□ 384
■ 384

6-54
24

■ 352
□ 416

6-55
72

■ 406
□ 362

6-56
42

□ 365
□ 128
▨ 165
■ 110

6-57
12

□ 448
■ 320

6-58
72

□ 256
□ 256
■ 256

6-59
9

□ 171
□ 597

6-60
26

□ 384
■ 384

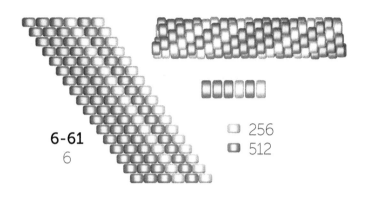

6-61
6

	256
	512

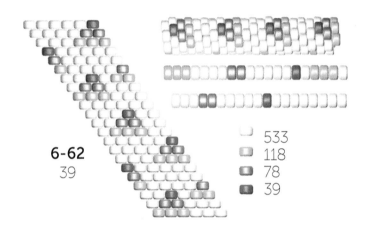

6-62
39

	533
	118
	78
	39

 6-63
39

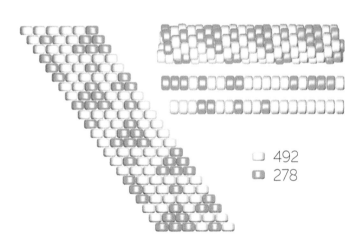

	492
	278

Seven-around tube patterns

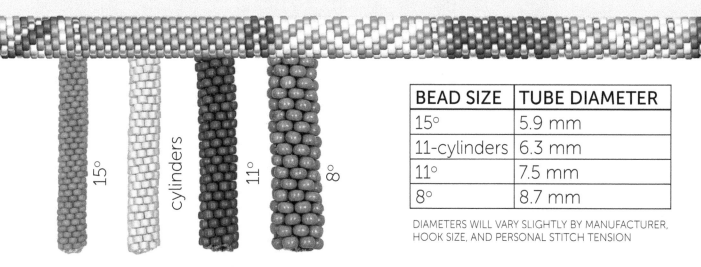

BEAD SIZE	TUBE DIAMETER
15°	5.9 mm
11-cylinders	6.3 mm
11°	7.5 mm
8°	8.7 mm

DIAMETERS WILL VARY SLIGHTLY BY MANUFACTURER, HOOK SIZE, AND PERSONAL STITCH TENSION

Seven-around tubes work up quickly, and just like six-around they self-support. Because the circumference number is odd, there are some unusual patterns that can be designed.

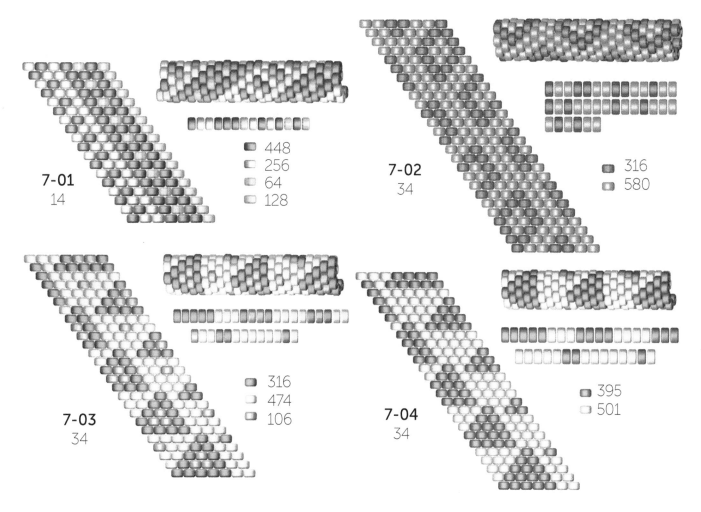

7-01
14

- 448
- 256
- 64
- 128

7-02
34

- 316
- 580

7-03
34

- 316
- 474
- 106

7-04
34

- 395
- 501

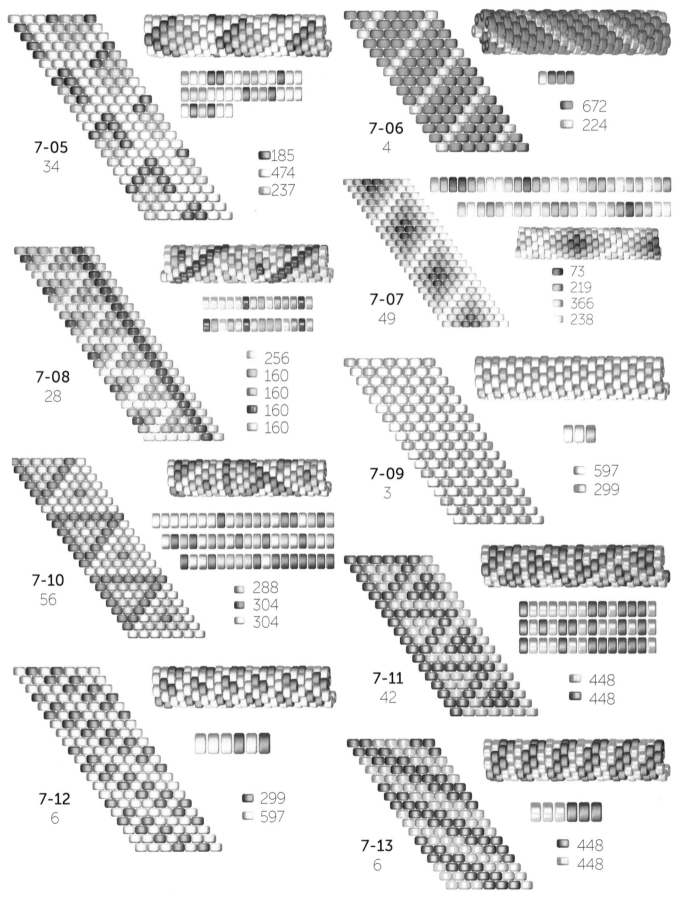

7-05
34

■ 185
□ 474
□ 237

7-06
4

■ 672
□ 224

7-07
49

■ 73
■ 219
□ 366
□ 238

7-08
28

□ 256
■ 160
■ 160
■ 160
□ 160

7-09
3

□ 597
■ 299

7-10
56

■ 288
■ 304
□ 304

7-11
42

□ 448
■ 448

7-12
6

■ 299
□ 597

7-13
6

■ 448
□ 448

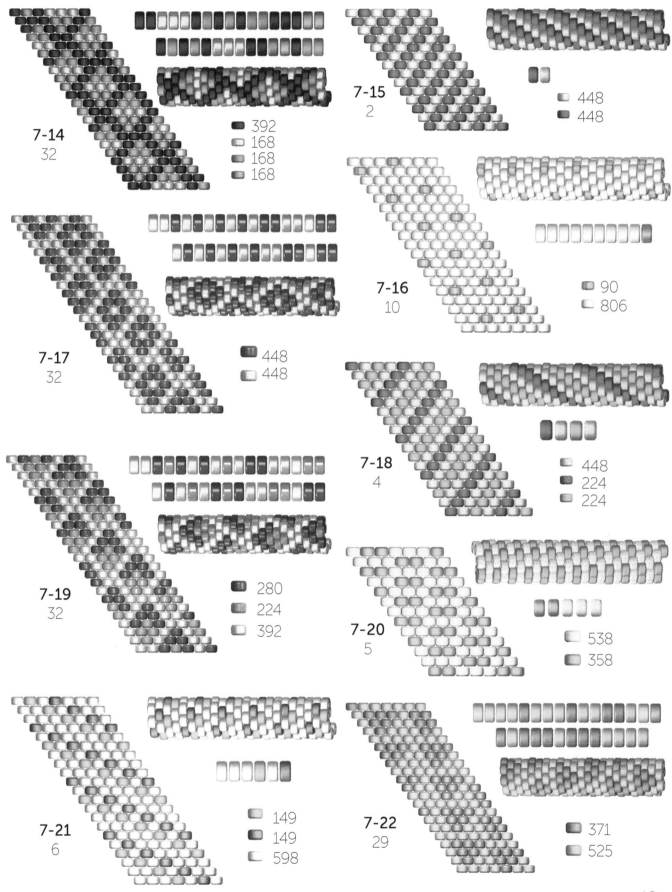

7-14
32

392
168
168
168

7-15
2

448
448

7-17
32

448
448

7-16
10

90
806

7-19
32

280
224
392

7-18
4

448
224
224

7-21
6

149
149
598

7-20
5

538
358

7-22
29

371
525

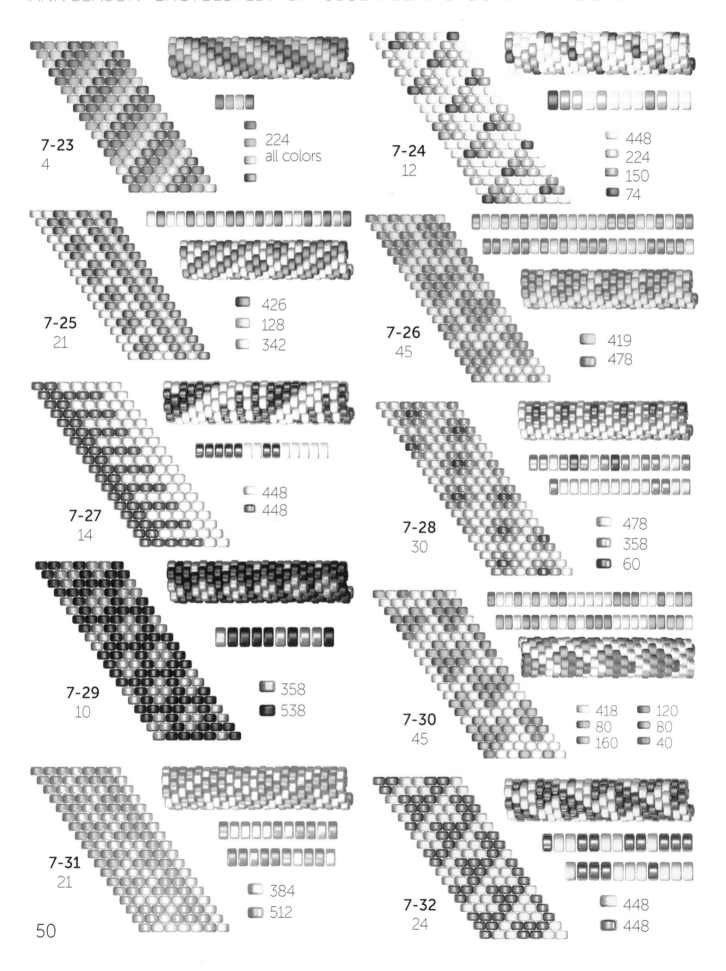

7-23
4

224
all colors

7-24
12

448
224
150
74

7-25
21

426
128
342

7-26
45

419
478

7-27
14

448
448

7-28
30

478
358
60

7-29
10

358
538

7-30
45

418   120
80   80
160   40

7-31
21

384
512

7-32
24

448
448

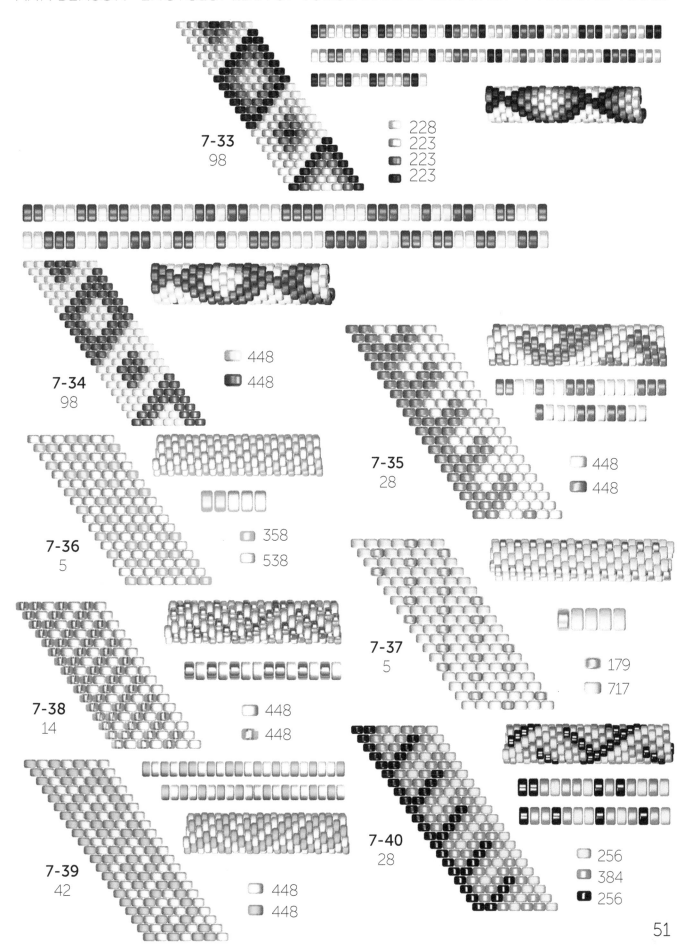

7-33
98

	228
	223
	223
	223

7-34
98

	448
	448

7-35
28

	448
	448

7-36
5

	358
	538

7-37
5

	179
	717

7-38
14

	448
	448

7-39
42

	448
	448

7-40
28

	256
	384
	256

Eight-around tube patterns

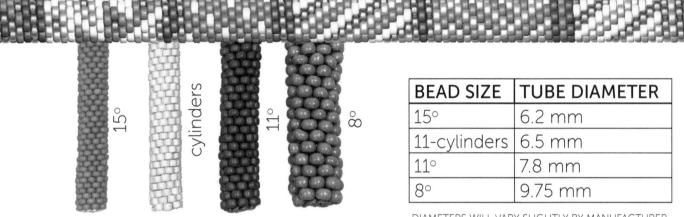

BEAD SIZE	TUBE DIAMETER
15°	6.2 mm
11-cylinders	6.5 mm
11°	7.8 mm
8°	9.75 mm

DIAMETERS WILL VARY SLIGHTLY BY MANUFACTURER, HOOK SIZE, AND PERSONAL STITCH TENSION

Eight-around patterns have good detail and a nice hand when crocheted; they are self-supporting, especially in the smaller bead sizes, and produce a nice bracelet tube.

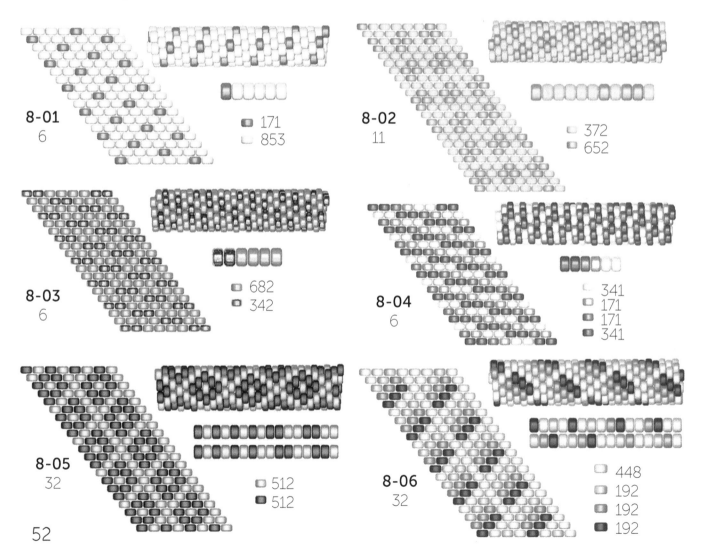

8-01
6

□ 171
□ 853

8-02
11

□ 372
□ 652

8-03
6

□ 682
□ 342

8-04
6

□ 341
□ 171
□ 171
□ 341

8-05
32

52

□ 512
□ 512

8-06
32

□ 448
□ 192
□ 192
□ 192

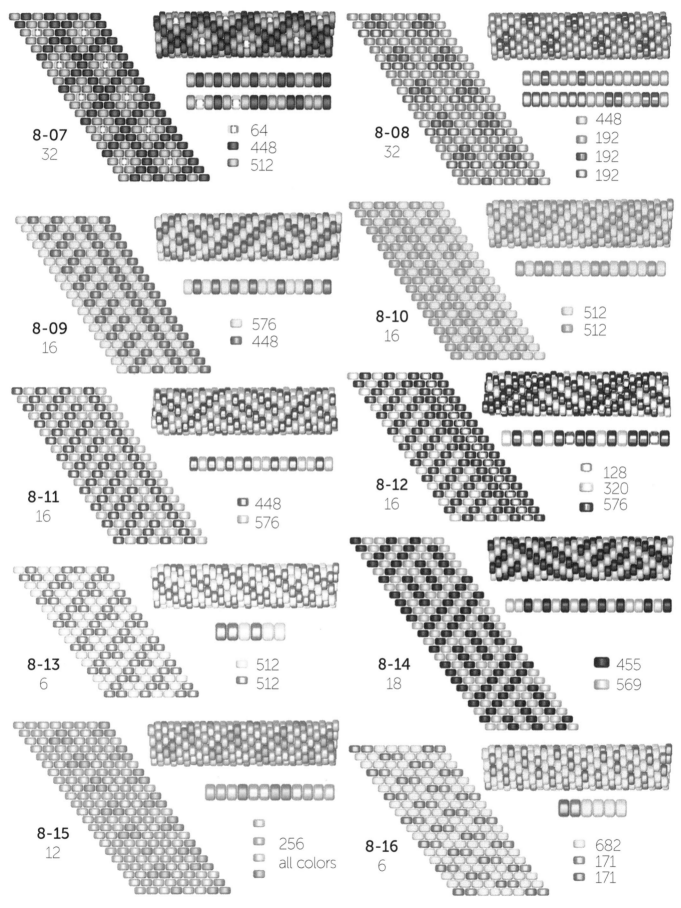

8-07
32

☐ 64
■ 448
☐ 512

8-08
32

☐ 448
☐ 192
■ 192
☐ 192

8-09
16

☐ 576
■ 448

8-10
16

☐ 512
☐ 512

8-11
16

■ 448
☐ 576

8-12
16

☐ 128
☐ 320
■ 576

8-13
6

☐ 512
☐ 512

8-14
18

■ 455
☐ 569

8-15
12

☐
☐ 256
☐ all colors
☐

8-16
6

☐ 682
☐ 171
☐ 171

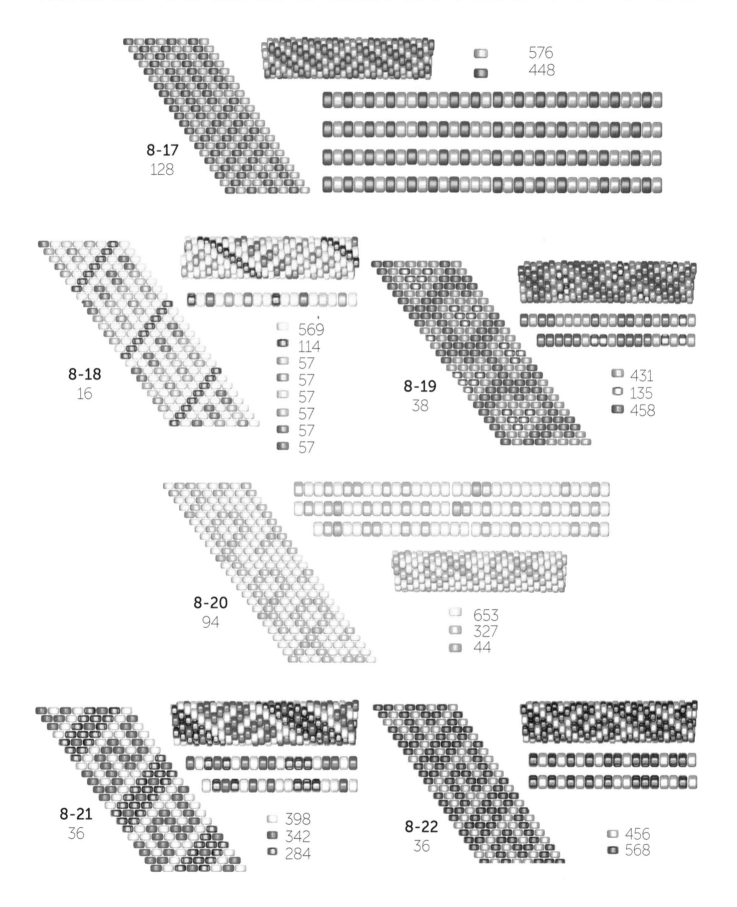

8-17
128

576
448

8-18
16

569
114
57
57
57
57
57
57

8-19
38

431
135
458

8-20
94

653
327
44

8-21
36

398
342
284

8-22
36

456
568

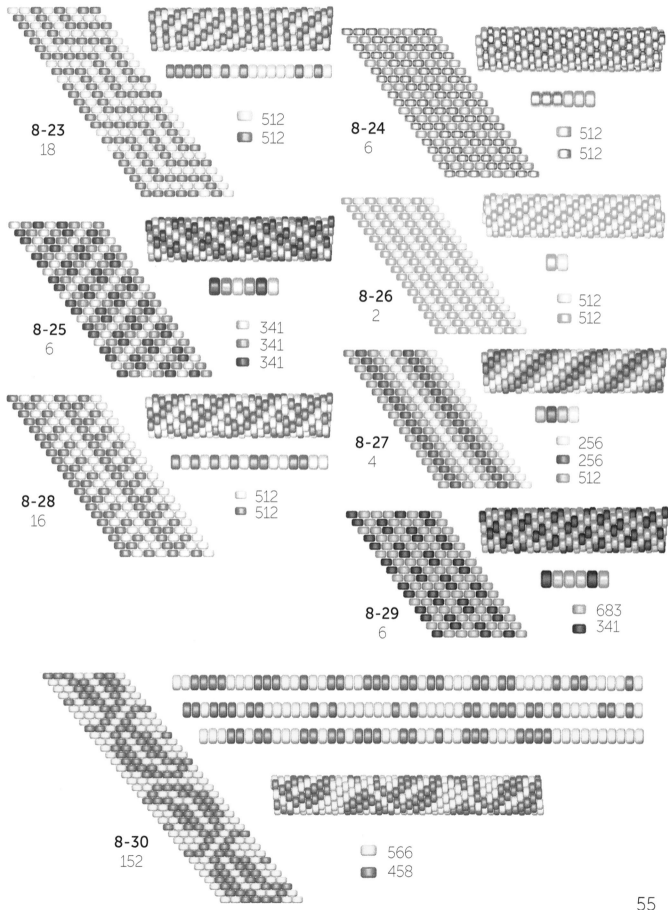

8-23
18

512
512

8-24
6

512
512

8-25
6

341
341
341

8-26
2

512
512

8-28
16

512
512

8-27
4

256
256
512

8-29
6

683
341

8-30
152

566
458

55

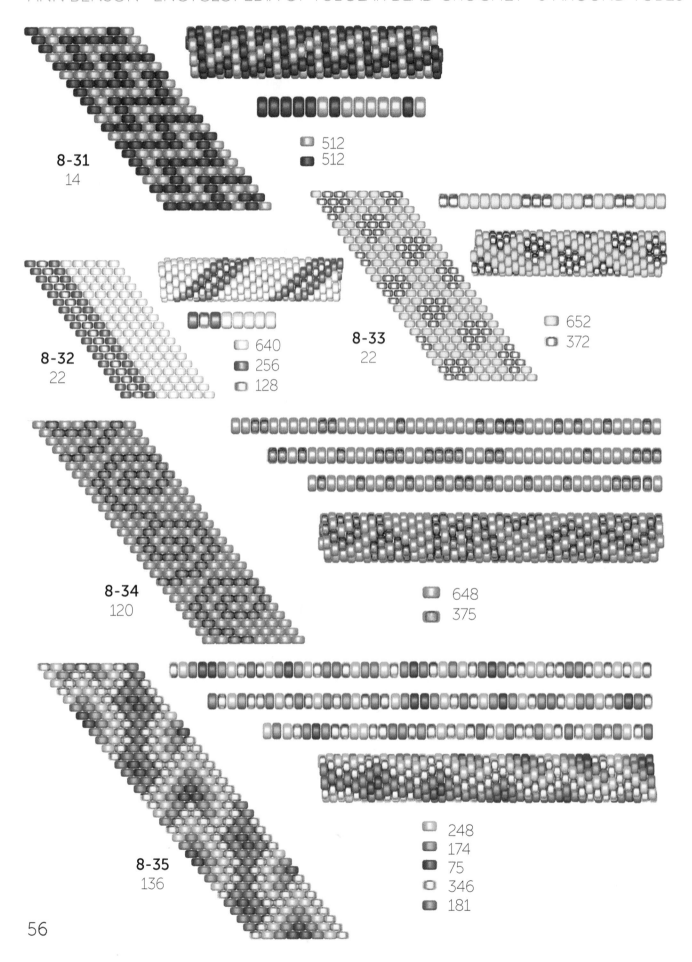

8-31
14

512
512

8-32
22

640
256
128

8-33
22

652
372

8-34
120

648
375

8-35
136

248
174
75
346
181

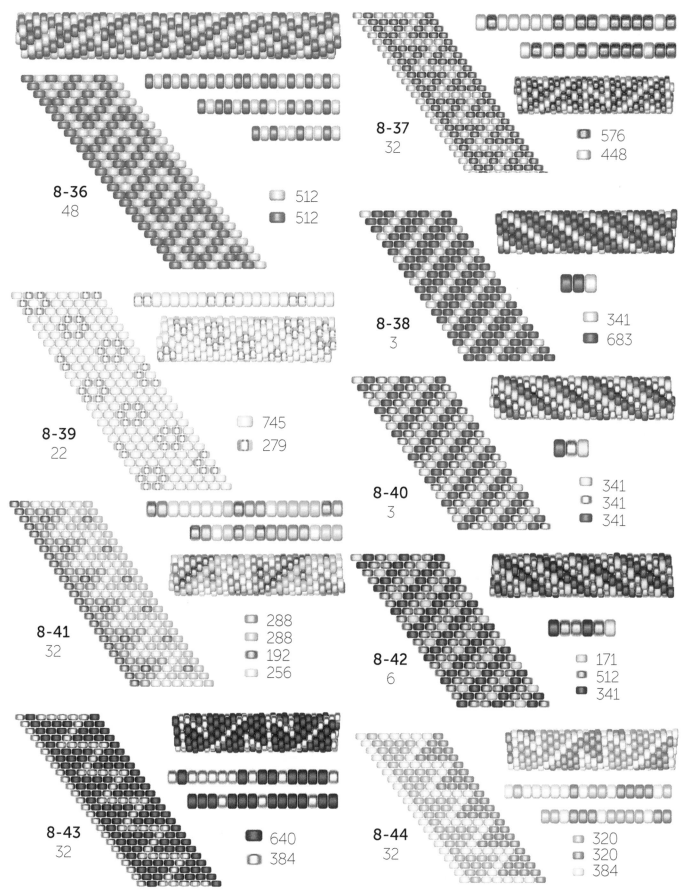

8-36
48

| | 512 |
| | 512 |

8-37
32

| | 576 |
| | 448 |

8-39
22

| | 745 |
| | 279 |

8-38
3

| | 341 |
| | 683 |

8-41
32

	288
	288
	192
	256

8-40
3

	341
	341
	341

8-42
6

	171
	512
	341

8-43
32

| | 640 |
| | 384 |

8-44
32

	320
	320
	384

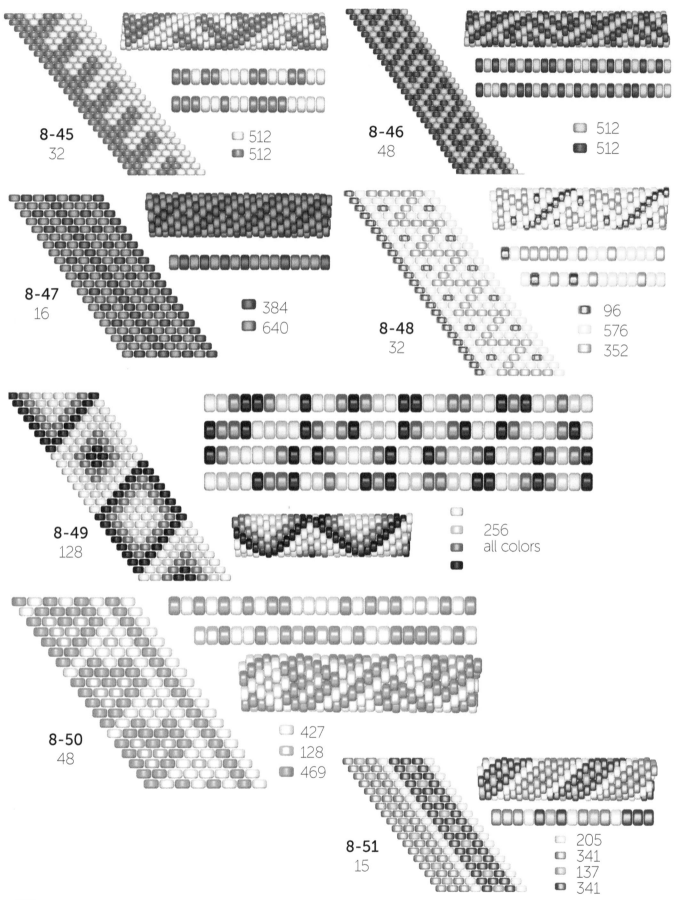

8-45
32

☐ 512
◼ 512

8-46
48

☐ 512
◼ 512

8-47
16

◼ 384
◻ 640

8-48
32

◻ 96
☐ 576
☐ 352

8-49
128

☐
☐ 256
◼ all colors
◼

8-50
48

☐ 427
☐ 128
◻ 469

8-51
15

☐ 205
◻ 341
☐ 137
◼ 341

Nine-around tube patterns

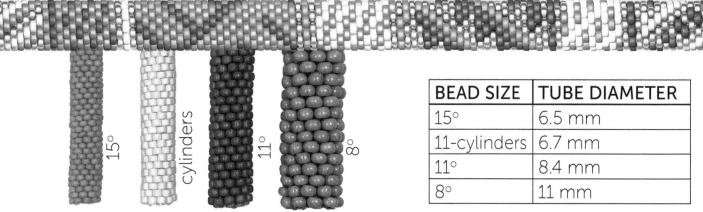

BEAD SIZE	TUBE DIAMETER
15°	6.5 mm
11-cylinders	6.7 mm
11°	8.4 mm
8°	11 mm

DIAMETERS WILL VARY SLIGHTLY BY MANUFACTURER, HOOK SIZE, AND PERSONAL STITCH TENSION

Patterns develop wonderfully in nine-around; geometric patterns work out nicely. In larger size beads (8° or larger) some tubes may collapse in on themselves, especially if your tension is loose, but you can add internal support to retain roundness.

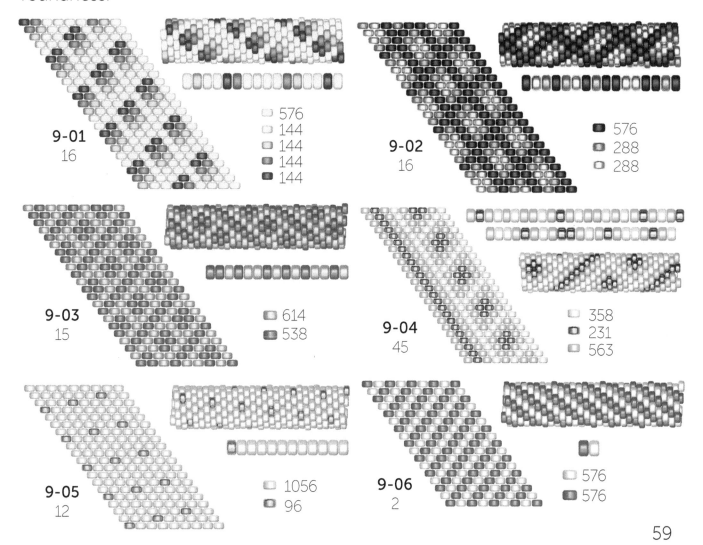

9-01
16

- 576
- 144
- 144
- 144
- 144

9-02
16

- 576
- 288
- 288

9-03
15

- 614
- 538

9-04
45

- 358
- 231
- 563

9-05
12

- 1056
- 96

9-06
2

- 576
- 576

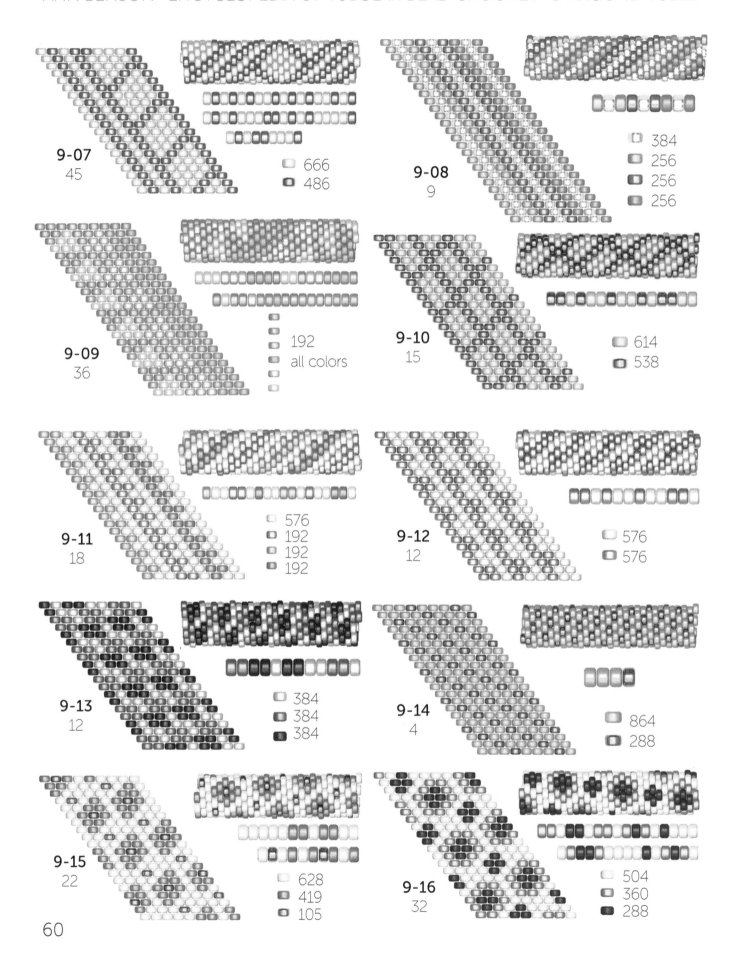

9-07
45

666
486

9-08
9

384
256
256
256

9-09
36

192
all colors

9-10
15

614
538

9-11
18

576
192
192
192

9-12
12

576
576

9-13
12

384
384
384

9-14
4

864
288

9-15
22

628
419
105

9-16
32

504
360
288

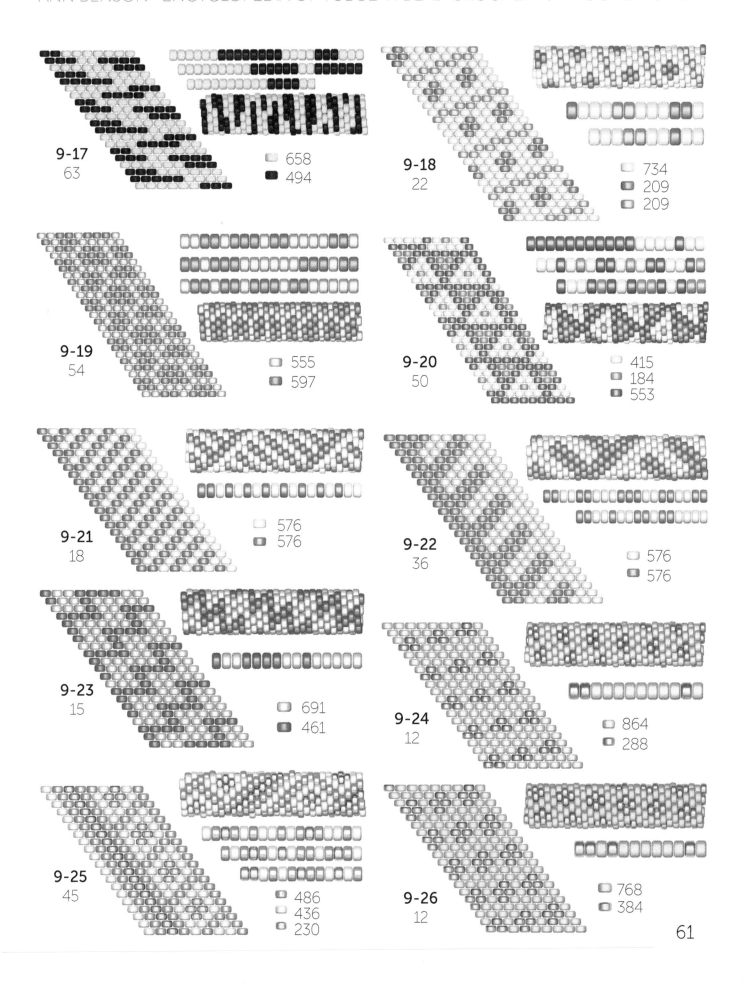

9-17
63

□ 658
■ 494

9-18
22

□ 734
□ 209
□ 209

9-19
54

□ 555
□ 597

9-20
50

□ 415
□ 184
□ 553

9-21
18

□ 576
□ 576

9-22
36

□ 576
□ 576

9-23
15

□ 691
□ 461

9-24
12

□ 864
□ 288

9-25
45

□ 486
□ 436
□ 230

9-26
12

□ 768
□ 384

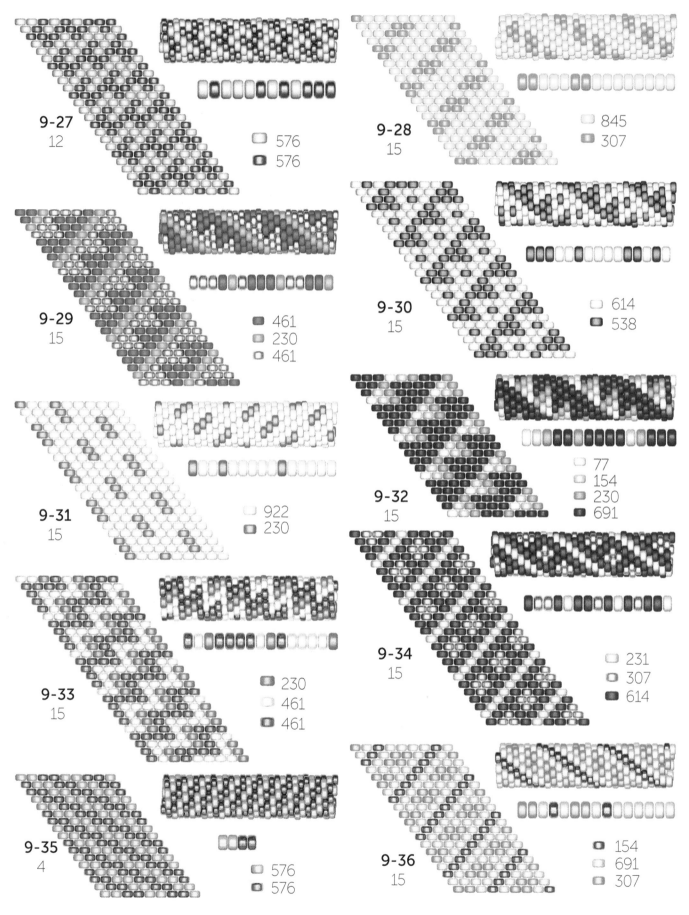

9-27
12

☐ 576
☐ 576

9-28
15

☐ 845
☐ 307

9-29
15

☐ 461
☐ 230
☐ 461

9-30
15

☐ 614
☐ 538

9-31
15

☐ 922
☐ 230

9-32
15

☐ 77
☐ 154
☐ 230
☐ 691

9-33
15

☐ 230
☐ 461
☐ 461

9-34
15

☐ 231
☐ 307
☐ 614

9-35
4

☐ 576
☐ 576

9-36
15

☐ 154
☐ 691
☐ 307

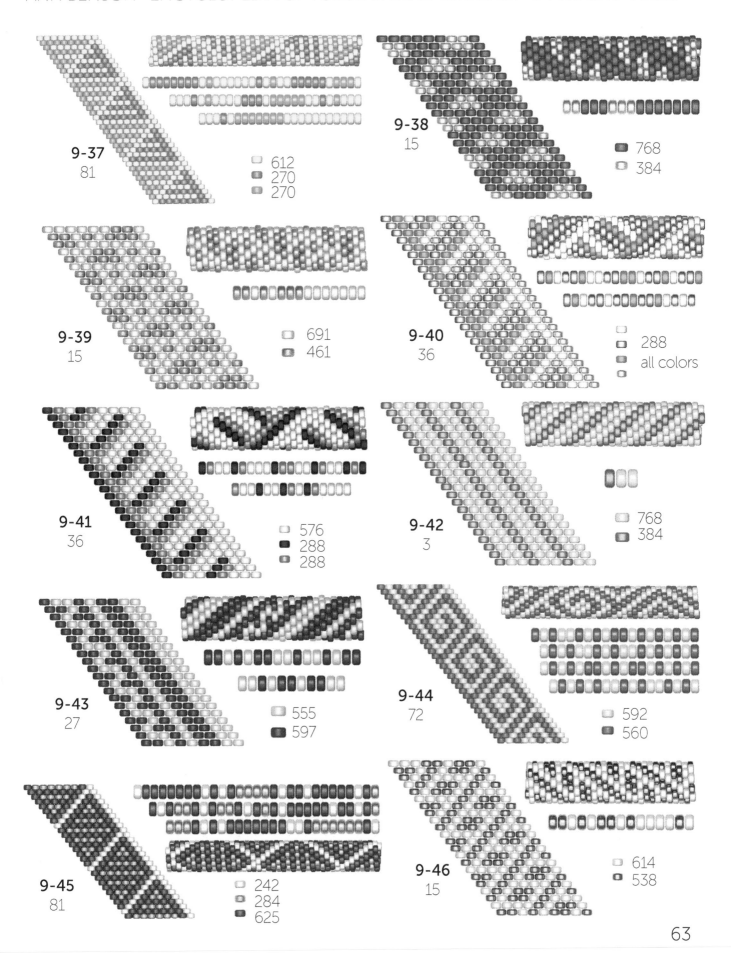

9-37
81

612
270
270

9-38
15

768
384

9-39
15

691
461

9-40
36

288
all colors

9-41
36

576
288
288

9-42
3

768
384

9-43
27

555
597

9-44
72

592
560

9-45
81

242
284
625

9-46
15

614
538

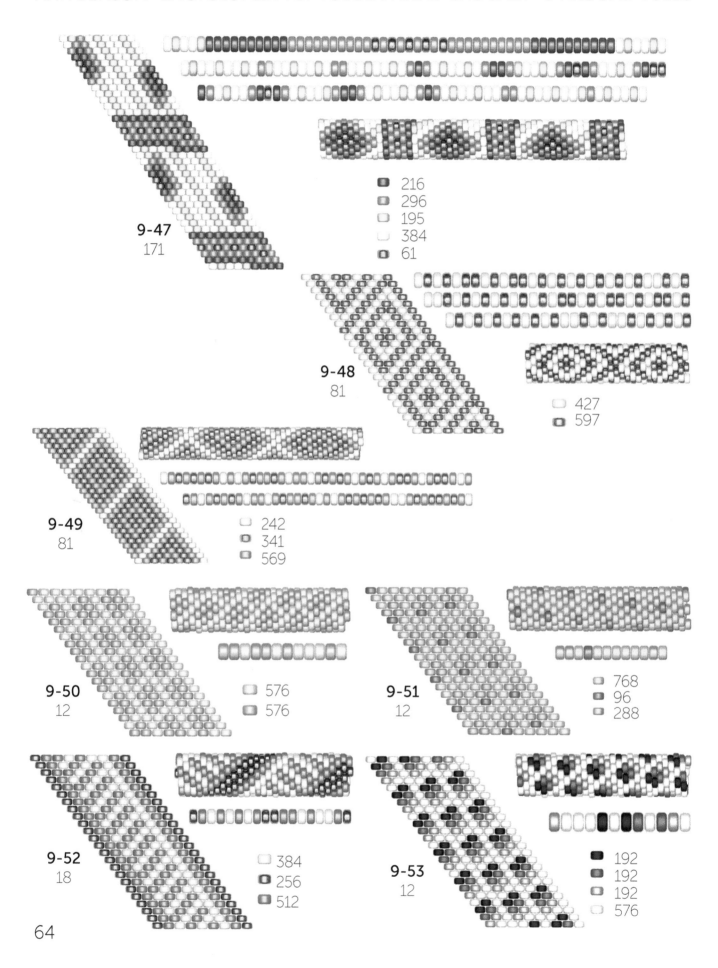

9-47
171

◼ 216
◼ 296
◻ 195
▢ 384
◼ 61

9-48
81

◻ 427
◼ 597

9-49
81

▢ 242
◼ 341
◼ 569

9-50
12

◻ 576
◼ 576

9-51
12

◻ 768
◼ 96
◻ 288

9-52
18

◻ 384
◼ 256
◼ 512

9-53
12

◼ 192
◼ 192
◻ 192
▢ 576

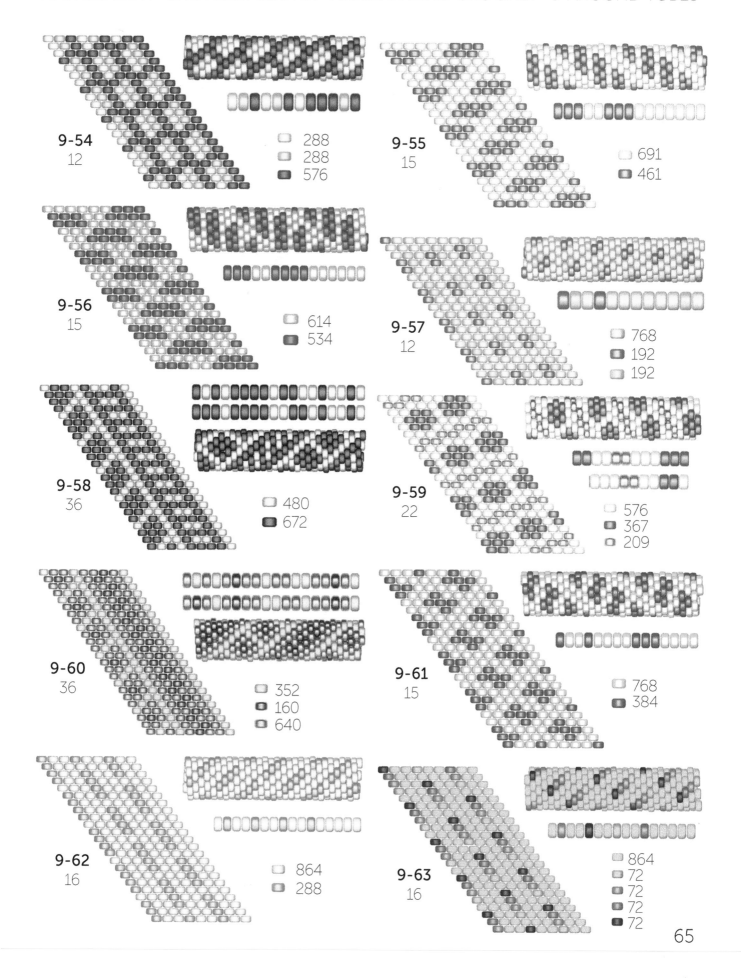

9-54
12

288
288
576

9-55
15

691
461

9-56
15

614
534

9-57
12

768
192
192

9-58
36

480
672

9-59
22

576
367
209

9-60
36

352
160
640

9-61
15

768
384

9-62
16

864
288

9-63
16

864
72
72
72
72

65

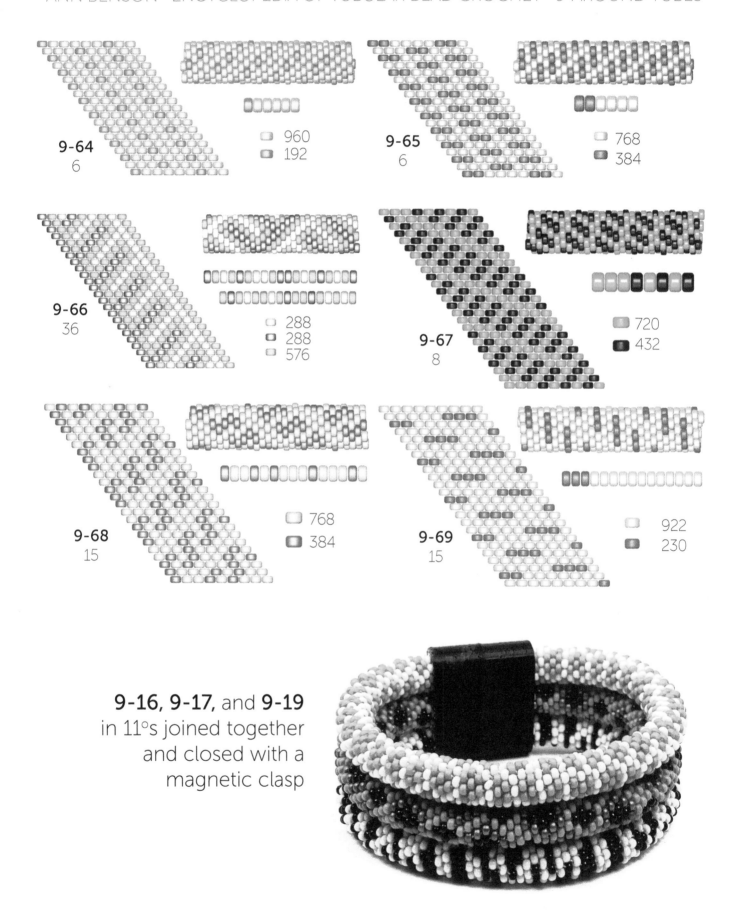

9-64
6

☐ 960
☐ 192

9-65
6

☐ 768
☐ 384

9-66
36

☐ 288
☐ 288
☐ 576

9-67
8

☐ 720
☐ 432

9-68
15

☐ 768
☐ 384

9-69
15

☐ 922
☐ 230

9-16, 9-17, and **9-19**
in 11°s joined together
and closed with a
magnetic clasp

Ten-around tube patterns

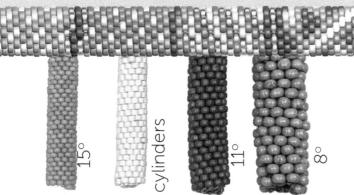

BEAD SIZE	TUBE DIAMETER
15°	6.9 mm
11-cylinders	7.4 mm
11°	9 mm
8°	12.5 mm

DIAMETERS WILL VARY SLIGHTLY BY MANUFACTURER, HOOK SIZE, AND PERSONAL STITCH TENSION

There's a breathtaking amount of area for design, graphical and pictorial. Small repeats emerge very cleanly. Take care with tension in ten-around as loosely crocheted tubes will likely collapse in on themselves, especially in beads 8° or larger. Tension should be even and consistent because variations will show up markedly in wider tubes. Heavier threads such as 10/2 or 8/2 perle cotton are recommended. It's difficult if not impossible to get a neat tube in 10-around with beads larger than 8°.

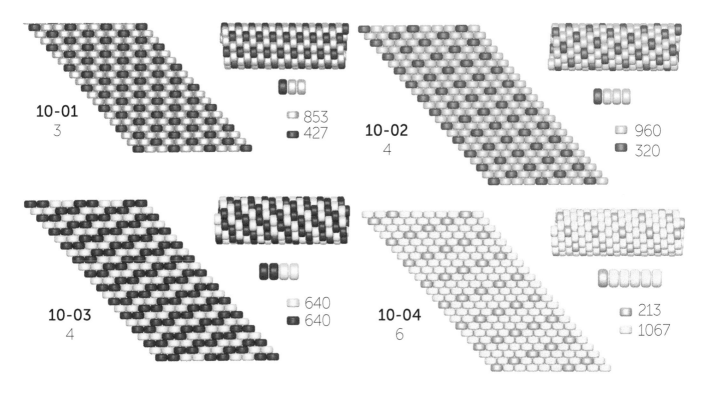

10-01
3

853
427

10-02
4

960
320

10-03
4

640
640

10-04
6

213
1067

Try combining the smaller more delicate patterns shown here with larger, bolder patterns for a unique look

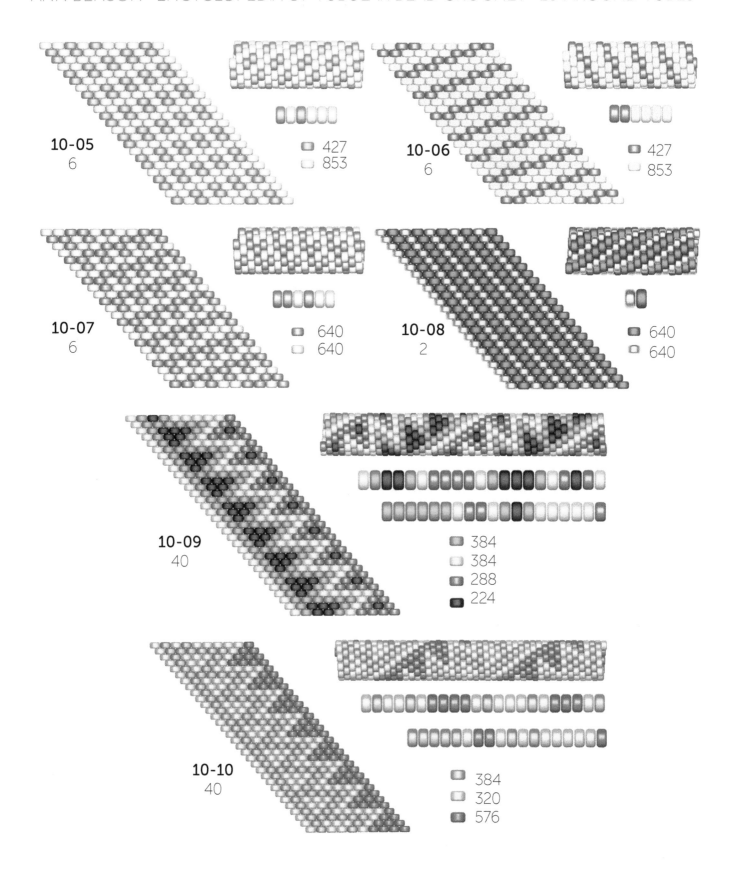

10-05
6

427
853

10-06
6

427
853

10-07
6

640
640

10-08
2

640
640

10-09
40

384
384
288
224

10-10
40

384
320
576

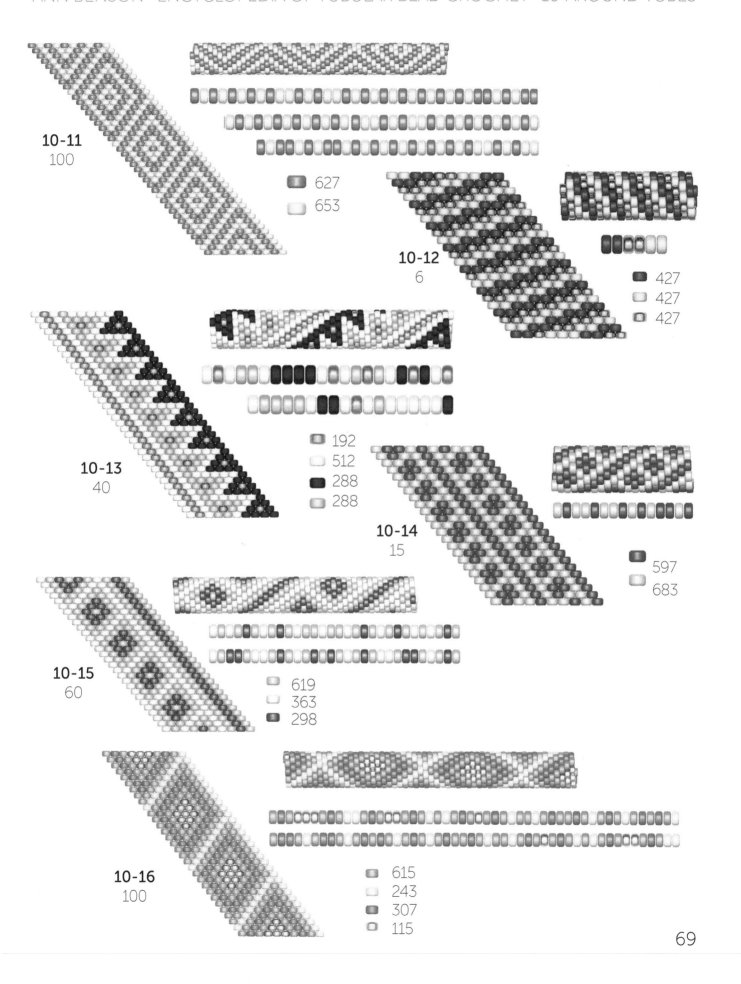

10-11
100

627
653

10-12
6

427
427
427

10-13
40

192
512
288
288

10-14
15

597
683

10-15
60

619
363
298

10-16
100

615
243
307
115

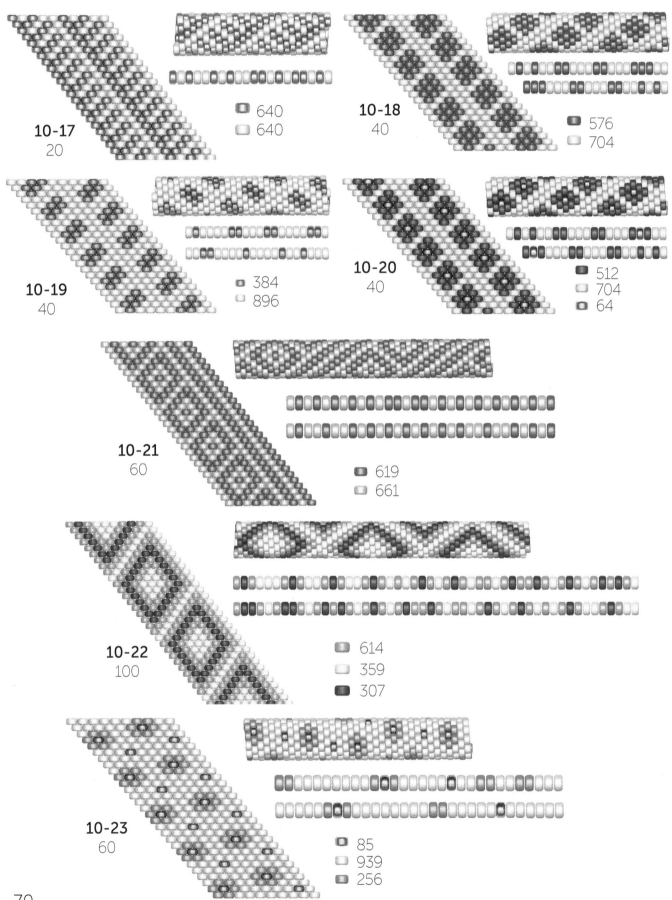

10-17
20

640
640

10-18
40

576
704

10-19
40

384
896

10-20
40

512
704
64

10-21
60

619
661

10-22
100

614
359
307

10-23
60

85
939
256

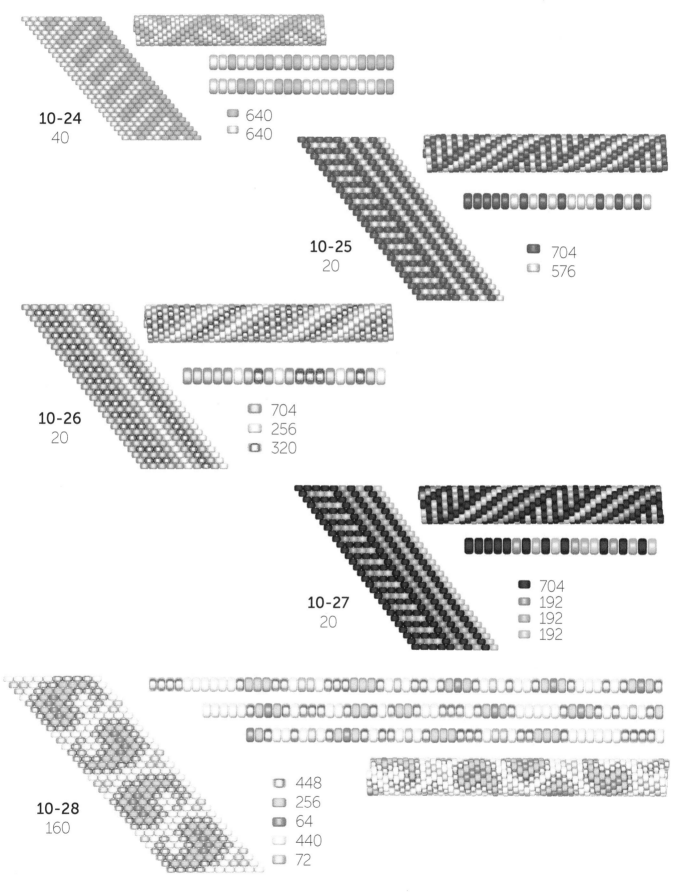

10-24
40

640
640

10-25
20

704
576

10-26
20

704
256
320

10-27
20

704
192
192
192

10-28
160

448
256
64
440
72

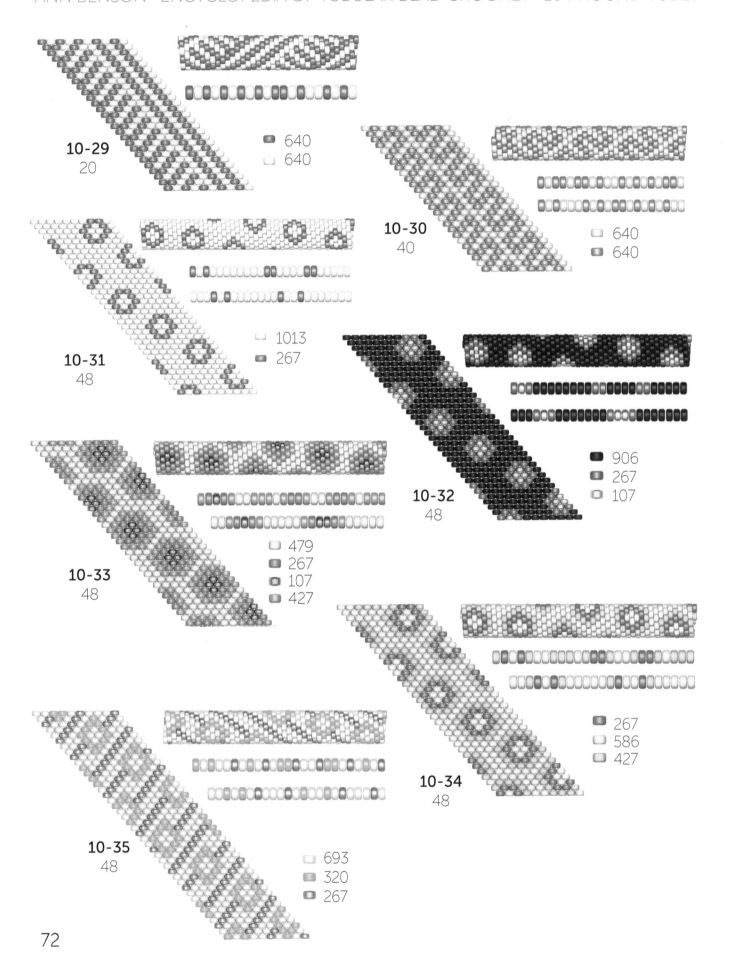

10-29
20

■ 640
□ 640

10-30
40

□ 640
■ 640

10-31
48

□ 1013
■ 267

10-32
48

■ 906
■ 267
□ 107

10-33
48

□ 479
■ 267
■ 107
■ 427

10-34
48

■ 267
□ 586
□ 427

10-35
48

□ 693
■ 320
■ 267

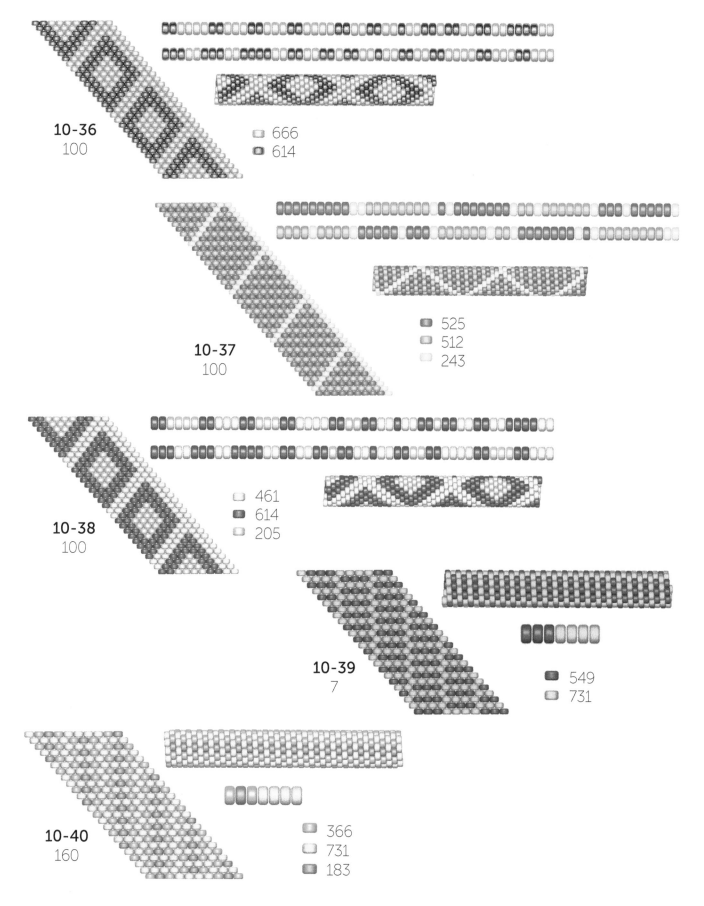

10-36
100

☐ 666
▣ 614

10-37
100

▪ 525
☐ 512
☐ 243

10-38
100

☐ 461
▪ 614
☐ 205

10-39
7

▪ 549
☐ 731

10-40
160

☐ 366
☐ 731
▣ 183

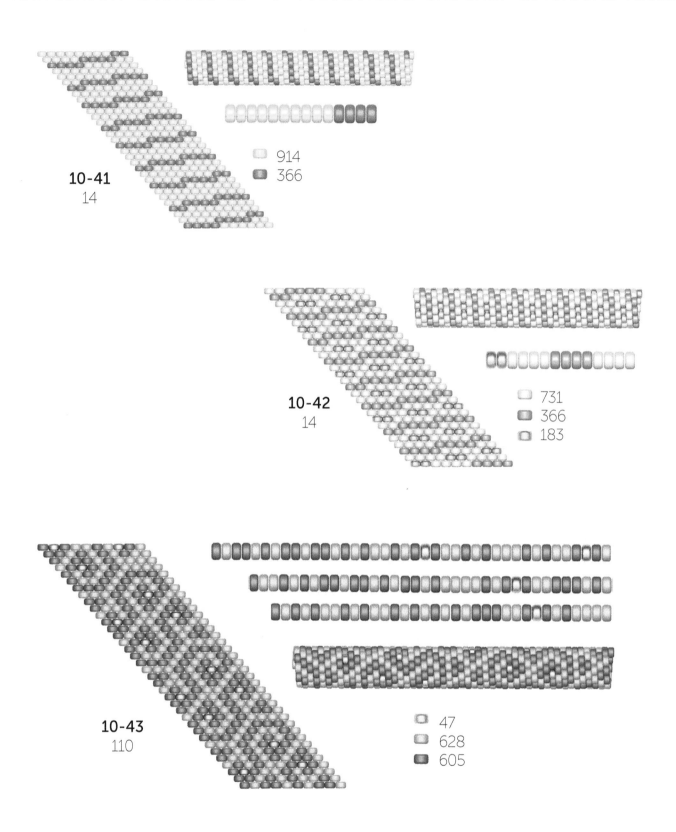

10-41
14

914
366

10-42
14

731
366
183

10-43
110

47
628
605

"Flat" tubes

Eight-around "flat" tube

They're not really flat.

The illusion of "flatness" is created when beads of a different color or size land in two opposite straight lines on a continuous tube.

The basic repeating pattern for a flat tube is a function of its circumference. The pattern will always be TWO TIMES THE CIRCUMFERENCE PLUS ONE. The graphic shown here for a ten-around flat design has twenty-one beads per repeat. Because these designs always have an odd number per repeat, one side will have "X" visible beads, while the other will have "X.5".

The overviews for six and seven around "flat" tubes shown below illustrate this oddity. Because you're creating a spiral, the beads do not land directly above each other; there's always a half-bead shift.

The half-bead shift

The six-around pattern has a thirteen bead repeat.

FLAT 6

◻ 118
◻ 650

The seven-around pattern has a fifteen-bead repeat

FLAT 7

◻ 118
◻ 778

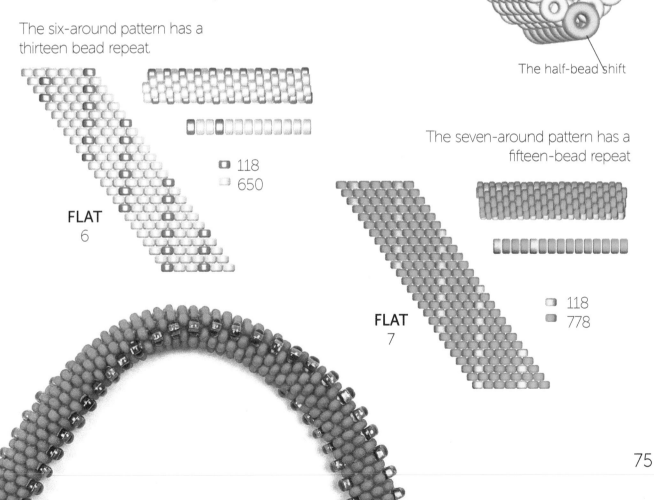

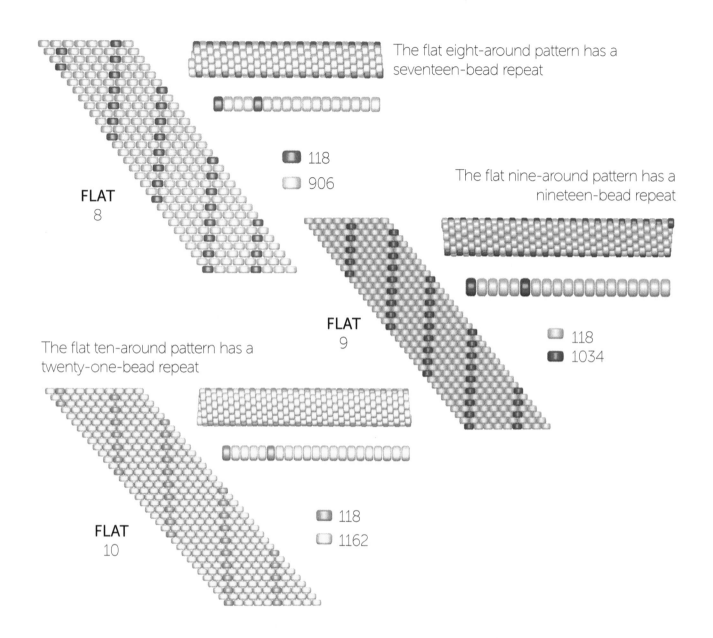

The flat eight-around pattern has a seventeen-bead repeat

■ 118
□ 906

The flat nine-around pattern has a nineteen-bead repeat

FLAT 8

FLAT 9

The flat ten-around pattern has a twenty-one-bead repeat

□ 118
■ 1034

FLAT 10

■ 118
□ 1162

Flat patterns can be reversible.

SIX-AROUND

SEVEN-AROUND

EIGHT-AROUND

NINE-AROUND

TEN-AROUND

Slight alterations in the pattern, with the same number of beads per repeat, will produce a tube with one color on one side and one color on the other. Shown with 6°s and 8°s, six-around.

Finishing

You may have already given some thought to this issue as part of your design planning process. You have a lot of choices, and most of them are very easy. Except of course for the dreaded Invisible Join. It can bring a 50-year crafter to his or her knees. But we'll demystify it shortly.

Roll-on finishing with a focal bead

You can use the crochet thread tails for this method, but it's better to use a really strong thread such as conso or strong nylon (never Fireline) because the thread will be subjected to friction. Secure the finishing thread within the fibers of the tube ends and bring it out in the center of the channel.

Be prepared to replace the finishing thread over the life of the bracelet.

Crochet one round of slip stitch without beads at the ending end.

At least two passes of thread in both directions are required for strength. Placing spacers between larger beads and caps will allow a smoother bend. Small caps may benefit from glue to hold their positions.

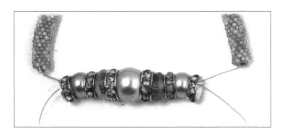

With a large span of beads, you may find it easier to work with two needles, one on each end. Doing so allows you to tighten both threads at the same time for a well-compressed span. In this example, crystal rondelles work well as caps.

Crocheted loop and bead

This technique allows the joining of two six-around tubes of bead crochet into one end, which is then reduced and continued as the main tube. The bead is attached at the ending end. You can continue the main tube in six, eight, or ten around tubes.

Load more beads than you think you'll need. Crochet a 6-around tube to a length that fill fit around your chosen closure bead. Pull out two yards of thread, then cut the thread and pull it through the last loop, Position the two ends together so the last stitch of the working end is next to the first stitch of the starting end as shown in A.

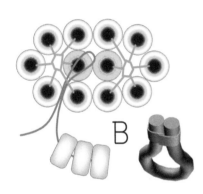

Tape the two ends together in this position (B). You'll need three rounds to establish the joint for ten and eight around, five rounds for six around. If you're continuing in ten around, add thirty beads; eight around, twenty-eight beads; six around, forty-two beads. Thread the required number of beads onto the two-yard end. Crochet around the ten outer beads (C). The beads of the starting end are already donut-positioned; it may take a bit of force to push the hook through and pass the bead to the far side of the hook. The beads of the finishing end will be tire-positioned correctly and no force will be necessary. Your "tube" will look like diagram C from the top.

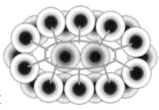

Work a second round of ten beads. If you're continuing ten-around, simply add one more round of ten, and then pull in a new thread with your main tube beads. For eight or six around, reduce this third round by stitching with no bead in the stitches shown with green beads in D. This completes the joint for eight around; pull in the thread with your main tube beads and continue.

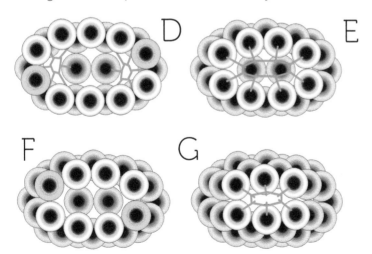

For six-around, crochet one round of the full eight (E), and then in the final round, reduce at the beads shown in green in F. Now you can continue in six-around as shown in G.

Wire finishing

Run a wire through the channel of your tube to attach a two-part clasp, or create a loop that is caught in a lobster claw on the other end.

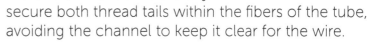

To prepare the tube: Make one round of unbeaded stitches at the end of the tube. Carefully secure both thread tails within the fibers of the tube, avoiding the channel to keep it clear for the wire.

You'll need:
Round nose pliers
Flat pliers
Wire cutters
Emery board or file
Two-part clasp
Decorative beads
24 gauge wire

To prepare the wire: Cut the wire at least three inches longer than the required length. Roll the wire on a hard flat surface to straighten it, then use an emery board or nail file to de-burr the ends. Rotate the wire as you run it through the tube.

ONE UNBEADED ROUND

END DE-BURRED WITH FILE
OR EMERY BOARD

Place your end decorations (in this case a cap and spacer) on the wire, then using round pliers, form a loop. Slip one end of the clasp on the loop. Wrap the wire around itself at least twice, then trim off the excess wire. Flatten the cut end with the flat-nose pliers. Before compressing the tube against the cap, place an optional dab of glue on the end of the tube.

Check the fit before adding the second part of the clasp. Compress or decompress the tube to fit the required length.

Wire finishing with a lobster claw is very similar, the only real difference being that the second loop does not have a "part" attached. The lobster claw hooks into the second loop. Be sure to size the loop so the claw can attach easily.

Loop and bead closure

This method of finishing is very simple and allows you to pick up bead colors in the decorative elements you choose. Great for necklaces; sizing can be adjusted by adding more decorative beads.

You'll need:
Large "button" bead
Decorative elements
Complementary seed beads that will accept multiple thread passes
Strong nylon beading thread.

Secure the crochet thread tails after making an unbeaded round of crochet at the end. Secure the nylon beading thread within the area that will be covered by decorative beads. Pick up the decorative beads and enough seed beads to form a loop that will fit over the large bead. There may be some trial and error in achieving the correct fit.

Make as many passes of thread as the beads will allow; secure the thread within the decorative area. When creating the beaded end, it should have roughly the same length for a harmonious appearance when worn. Be prepared to replace the thread from time to time over the life of the piece.

Magnetic clasps

Good-quality magnetic clasps are a wonderful method for finishing a crocheted bracelet or necklace. Choose a clasp with an INSIDE diameter that is just slightly larger than (or even the same as) the OUTSIDE diameter of your tube. A tube with an outside diameter of 8mm (about 5/16") will likely fit into a clasp with an 8mm inside diameter if your tension isn't so tight that the tube is rigid.

Use STRONG glue such as E6000 or Aleene's Glass and Bead glue. NEVER use a water-soluble glue. ALWAYS allow the glue to dry for at least six hours (or longer if the manufacturer recommends that).

IMPORTANT: Allow a bit of slack in your sizing; as you move your wrist, the expansion and contraction of your muscles will pop the magnets apart if the bracelet it too tight.

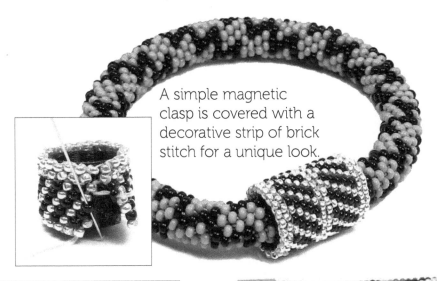

A simple magnetic clasp is covered with a decorative strip of brick stitch for a unique look.

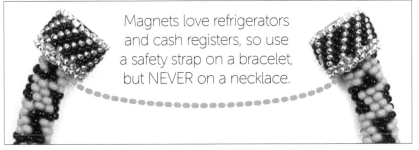

Magnets love refrigerators and cash registers, so use a safety strap on a bracelet, but NEVER on a necklace.

MAGNETIC CLASP ON A DOUBLE-EURO BEAD CROCHET BRACELET

In this example, four separate tubes are joined within a long magnetic clasp. The tubes are first stitched together through the assembled width with an invisible thread; you can incorporate decorative edge beads on the outer tubes in this step as shown here.

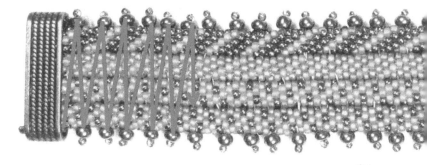

81

Invisible join finishing
Do not be afraid.

Two-sided "flat" tube
joined invisibly

In this elegant but somewhat daunting finishing method, one end of the tube is joined perfectly to the other end in a continuous circle with no visible start or end. The resulting bracelet can be rolled smoothly onto the wrist and is comfortable to wear.

Simple 6-around
repeating pattern
joined invisibly

In order for the join to succeed, your tube must be crocheted in FULL PATTERN REPEATS. In other words, you started your tube with the first bead of your chosen repeat and ended your tube with the last bead of that repeat.

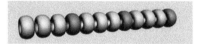

Three repeats of the 3-1 pattern are shown here. When crocheted 6-around, the dotted pattern emerges.

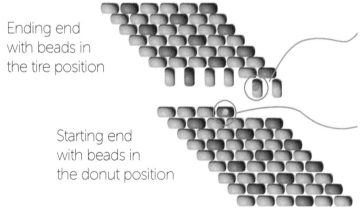

Ending end
with beads in
the tire position

Starting end
with beads in
the donut position

The first bead threaded is the last bead crocheted. Do NOT make one round of unbeaded stitches; the beads must be in the tire position.

The last bead threaded is the first bead crocheted. Secure the starting thread tail within the fibers of the tube and trim; do not run the thread through any bead holes.

Clear at least twelve inches (12") of unstitched thread of any remaining beads and cut the end thread. Secure the thread tail by running the cut end through the last loop on your hook.

Invisible join in progress

Put a needle onto the 12" tail and run it back into the fibers of the last couple of rounds. Reverse direction and bring it out of the hole of the last bead you crocheted INTO (the last donut position bead, shown red). Test first to be sure your needle will fit through the bead hole. This is the one and only time in this process that your thread will go through the hole in a bead.

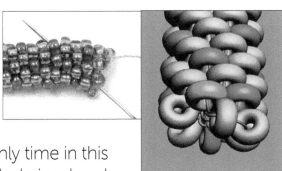

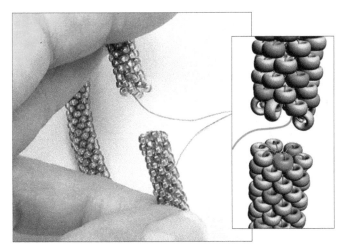

Align the end and start of the tube as shown here. This position is unfortunately known as the "cigarette hold", where the index and middle fingers hold one end of the tube and the thumb and ring finger hold the other end of the tube.

Follow the red thread path; dark blue dots indicate the thread that holds each bead in place on the tube. The thread must go in this specific path for the joint to appear seamless. Try not to pierce the thread itself, but rather run the needle through the loop that holds the bead so there is no distortion when you tighten the thread. This diagram shows all threads still loose; in reality, you will tighten the thread after each stitch.

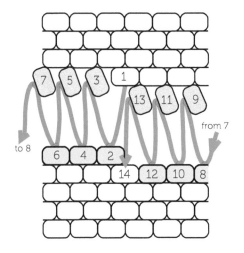

The beads shift position as you work around the tube. Tighten each attachment as you proceed.

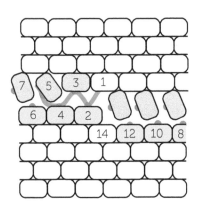

83

Invisible join complete

The join becomes cleaner as you progress. If an errant bead pops out, your thread may not be tight enough. Try to keep the tension even on all the attachments. To finish the join, repeat the first attachment over itself.

Secure the thread tail within the fibers of the tube; make back and forth passes but do not pull too tightly on the thread. To trim, pull on the tail slightly and cut it very close to the beads, then massage the tube so any visible cut end disappears within the tube. The join is complete. Well done!

Adding internal support to a tube

Support can be introduced during the crochet process using thin piping. Masking tape around the working end is recommended. Ease the support forward as you progress so it's always a bit outside the tube.

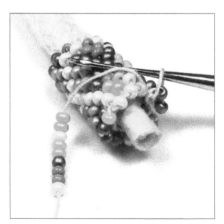

Or a fiber bundle can be pulled through the tube with a wire hook and trimmed to fit the tube precisely. Stitch the trimmed ends back and forth a few times to stabilize the fibers and add glue to the ends of the tube to keep the fibers in place. Trim them without cutting any crochet threads, then insert the end into the clasp or cap.

Designing your own

I have never used bead crochet software, so I can't recommend one. As of this publication, I use a trial-and-error method to work out patterns in Adobe Illustrator, but coloring in design blanks will work beautifully if you don't wish to sink to my nerd level.

You're designing for a spiral, so the repeats will not just line up alongside each other; they must continue uninterrupted for the desired length. The repeat "dips" one row down from the original. The design blanks on the following pages have two repeats beyond the original, one in red, one in blue, correctly aligned to the original tube, which is bold-outlined.

The blanks have 100 rows (rounds) but if you need more you can copy, cut and tape them together. They are slightly distorted narrower to fit on the page so do your math based on the number of rows/rounds you need rather than on the size you measure on the page.

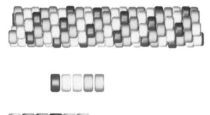

This 6-around pattern has a five-bead repeat. Shown below are three iterations of the flat pattern correctly aligned for a spiral. The original is full-color and the two subsequent patterns are faded.

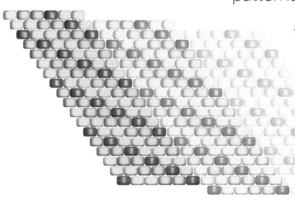

You can see at left how the overviews align, stepped down one row each time. In designing complex patterns, there can be quite a lot of trial and error. You have to think "spirally" though you're designing on a flat chart.

When your overview is ready for threading, start at the bottom left and load beads in order from left to right. Then move up one row and thread those beads from left to right. Continue working upward, left to right, until the pattern is threaded to the desired length.

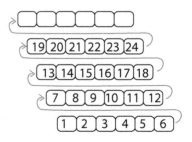

Five-around design blank

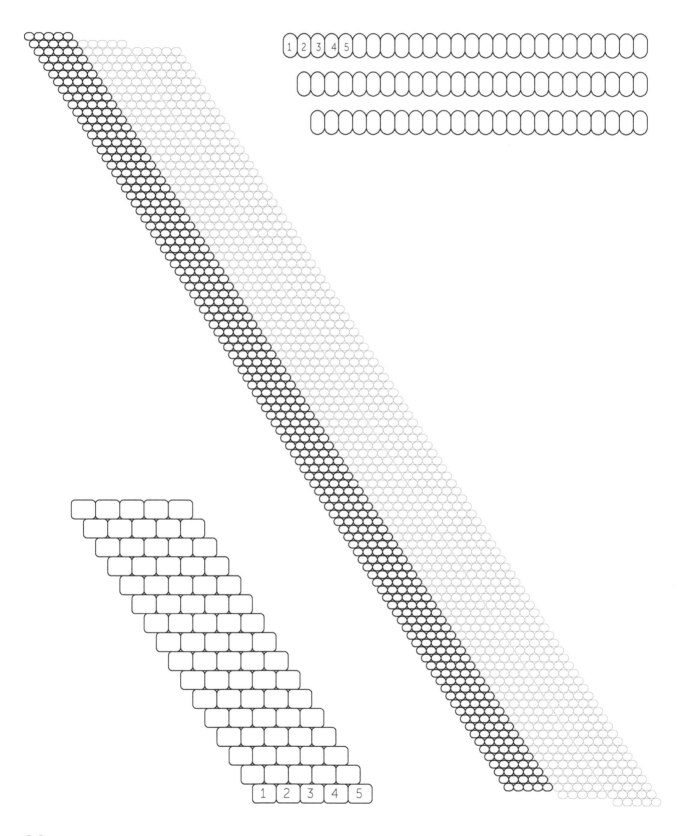

Six-around design blank

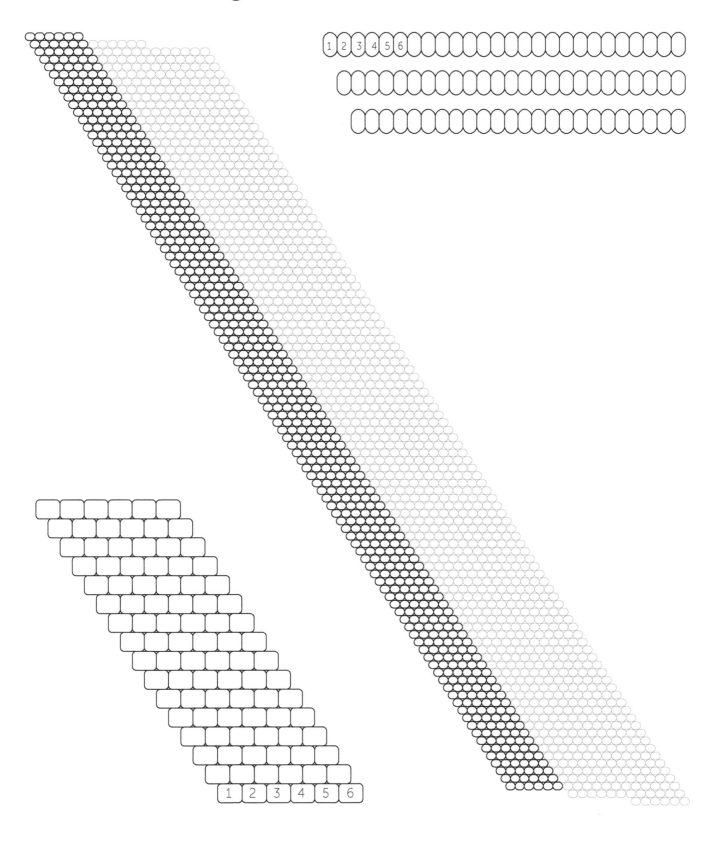

Seven-round design blank

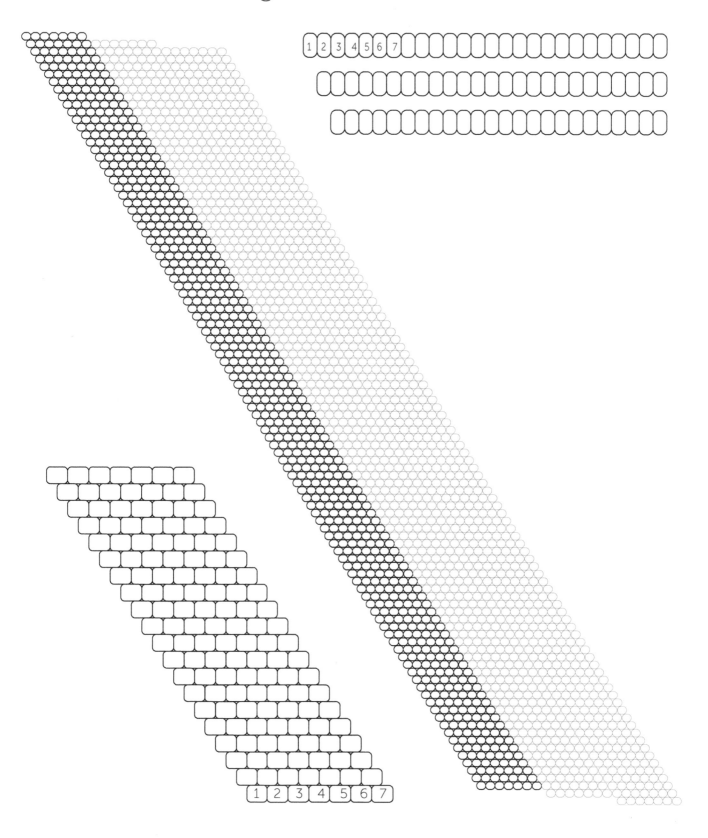

Eight-around design blank

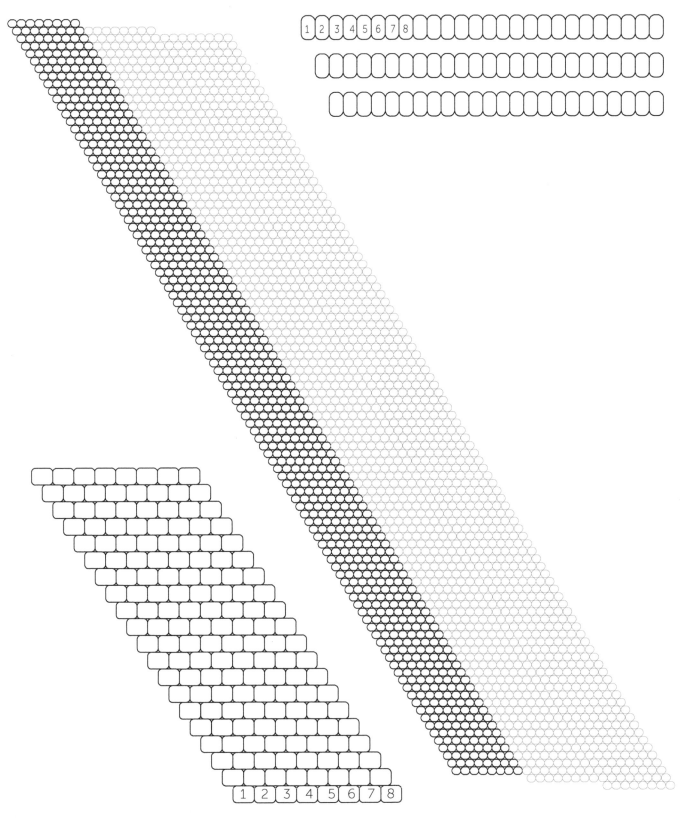

Nine-around design blank

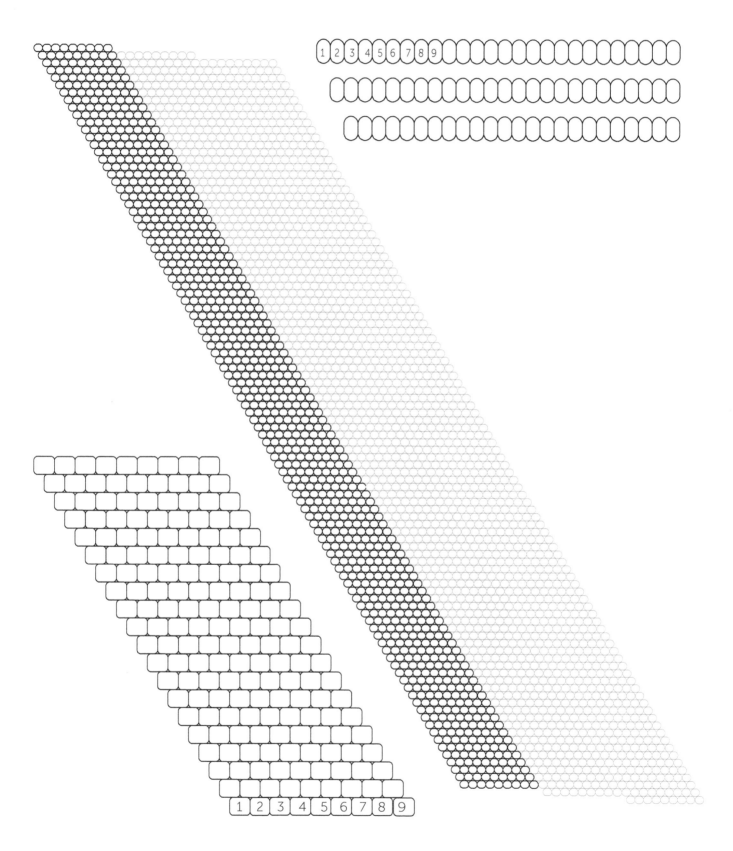

Ten around design blank

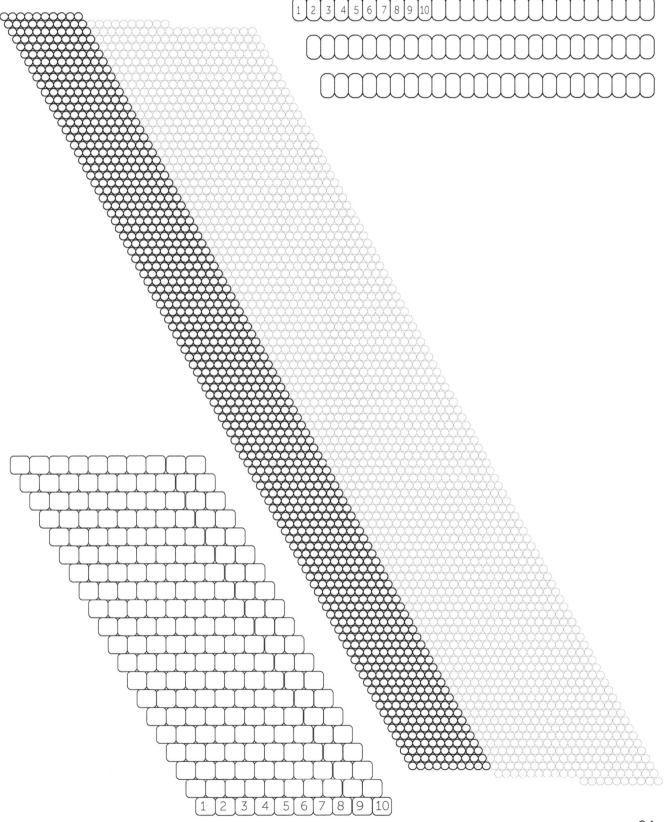

Freshwater pearl "flat" bracelet with tourmaline
drops and Swarovski bicone crystals, wire
finishing with a lobster claw closure

Resources

MATERIALS

Because crafting suppliers regrettably go in and out of business with much more rapidity than we'd like, specific sources are not listed here. There is a sourcing page available on my web site:

annbensonbeading.com

I will attempt to keep this page updated on a regular basis.

TUTORIALS

Video and print tutorials are plentiful on YouTube, Vimeo, and on specific independently operated sites. These will be noted on my resources page on annbensonbeading.com. Additionally, I maintain a large library of tutorial videos on my own Ann Benson/Beads East YouTube channel.

Print tutorials are available for free download on annbensonbeading.com.

SOFTWARE/APPS

The following software and apps were used in the creation of this book: Adobe InDesign, Adobe Illustrator, Adobe PhotoShop, Maxon Cinema 4D, Microsoft Word, Cochenille Stitchpainter Gold

GROUPS

Social media groups dedicated to specific beading techniques are plentiful. If you would like to have information posted about your group, or if you'd like me to join your group, please contact me through the contact page at annbensonbeading.com.

PERMISSIONS

Designs included in this book may be used to create crocheted items for resale without attribution.

"Design your own" blanks may be copied and reproduced for personal use.

Teachers wishing to use materials and tutorials should contact me directly through annbensonbeading.com; permission for teachers to use my material is rarely denied when attribution guidelines are observed.

No part of this book may be reproduced for resale under any circumstances. Designs in this book may not be used as part of a kit. Violators of these restrictions will be prosecuted to the full extent of the law.

Toho 8° 13F matte transparent light blue and Czech 8° 01710 silk silver in 6-around pattern (**6-22**), filigree caps with a sea glass focal bead in simple roll-on finishing

Index

From the author:

I welcome your polite comments and criticisms, and eagerly seek corrections! Please contact me through annbensonbeading.com with suggestions, errata, and other concerns.

Please feel free to review any of my beading books and novels on your purchase platform such as Amazon, Etsy, Barnes and Noble, and Kobo, or any other place where my books are sold.

Czech and Japanese 11°s, crocheted 8-around (**8-52**), with a vintage fern-patterned 18mm button bezeled in single beaded crochet, secured with a 6-around bead crocheted loop closure (**6-22**)

About the author

Ann Benson is an internationally acclaimed designer of beading, needle arts, and weaving, active for over fifty years in the crafting world. She is a renowned expert on all forms of bead crochet and bead embroidery, and is recognized for the accuracy and clarity of her directions and tutorials. She maintains a YouTube library of dozens of video tutorials and on-line classes, and a catalog of downloadable print tutorials on annbensonbeading.com. This encyclopedia is her ninth beading book.

Ann is also a Random House novelist, with five published novels.

She is the mother of two fabulous grown women and the grandmother of seven delightful children. She lives in Port Orange, Florida in the winter, and on Cape Cod in the summer, with her husband, retired police detective Gary Frost.

Japanese 15°s, crocheted 10-around **(10-28)** on Cebelia 30-weight using size 11/12 hook, with filigree caps, daisy spacers and turquoise focal bead in simple roll-on finishing

Chain stitch bracelet with loops of mixed 15°s, 11°s, and 8°s, on Conso nylon, with turquoise button and loop closure

Novels by Ann Benson

The Plague Trilogy
The Plague Tales

The Burning Road

The Physician's Tale

Stand-alone novels
Thief of Souls

Ambrosia

I welcome your reviews on your purchase platform.
Books can only get better when they are thoroughly
and thoughtfully reviewed!

Two tubular bead crochet bracelets
with crocheted loop closure, along
with one Double/Euro bead crochet
bracelet with a magnetic clasp